The German Influence on English Education

THE STUDENTS LIBRARY OF EDUCATION

The German Influence on English Education

by W. H. G. Armytage
Professor of Education
University of Sheffield

LONDON

ROUTLEDGE & KEGAN PAUL

NEW YORK: HUMANITIES PRESS

First published 1969
by Routledge & Kegan Paul Ltd
Broadway House, 68–74 Carter Lane
London, E.C.4

Printed in Great Britain
by Willmer Brothers Limited
Birkenhead, Cheshire

SBN 7100 6281 8

THE STUDENTS LIBRARY OF EDUCATION has been designed to meet the needs of students of Education at Colleges of Education and at University Institutes and Departments. It will also be valuable for practising teachers and educationists. The series takes full account of the latest developments in teacher-training and of new methods and approaches in education. Separate volumes will provide authoritative and up-to-date accounts of the topics within the major fields of sociology, philosophy and history of education, educational psychology, and method. Care has been taken that specialist topics are treated lucidly and usefully for the non-specialist reader. Altogether, the Students' Library of Education will provide a comprehensive introduction and guide to anyone concerned with the study of education, and with educational theory and practice.

J. W. TIBBLE

One group of books, in the history section of the series, discusses the influence of certain foreign countries on English education. It is not only German educationists, for instance, Froebel and Herbart, who have had a lasting influence on practice in Britain, but also German scientists and technologists, philosophers, sociologists and historians.

The story of the interplay between the two countries is a fascinating one, and Professor Armytage describes not only the impact of German innovations on this country, but also the influence of the many émigrés who came to this country after 1848, in the late nineteenth century, and again in the 1930's. He also reminds us that, not so long ago, Prussia was the Mecca of both English and American educationists.

In bringing this material together, Professor Armytage has broken new ground. This book cannot fail to stimulate fresh thinking about the way in which our own system of education has developed, and about the factors which have brought about change.

B. SIMON

'Truly, much humbug has been played off by literary men—unwittingly no doubt, for they themselves were sincere dupes-upon the pious and benevolent feelings of the European public, with regard to the excellence of the Prussian educational system . . . In their admiration of the wheels and machinery, these literary men have forgotten to look under the table and see what kind of web this was producing.'

(Laing, 1842, 230–1)

Contents

When I first lectured on this subject some twenty-one years ago at the University of Bonn, the two standard texts in this field were those of F. Althaus (1873) and K. H. Schaible (1885). Since then, in preparing further lectures for German lektors and lektorin and for undergraduate and graduate students at the University of Sheffield, other interpretations have come my way, notably those of Friedrich Schneider (1943), K. Dockhorn (1950 and 1954) and W. Fischer (1951), together with the valuable source book of Dr. Hermann Ody (1959): all in German. Two studies in English by George Haines IV (1957, 1958) and P. W. Musgrave (1967) have also appeared, so it seemed convenient, in view of a recommendation of the Robbins Committee (1963, p. 92), that a brief synopsis of the subject be issued for those who wished to correlate the study of German with that of Education. Further help to such students can be found listed in the *Cambridge Bibliography of English Literature* (1940) vols. ii pp. 50–65 and iii pp. 26–38, 55 and v pp. 376–8. That, and the bibliography appended at the end, should afford plenty of opportunities for individual studies in this field.

W.H.G.A.

1

Protestantism and Economic Penetration

Its cradle: Wittenburg

The first German university to be sanctioned by the Emperor, and not the Pope, was Wittenberg. Its founder, the elector of Saxony, also amassed in the church thousands of relics in the hope of making his dull Saxon town a place of pilgrimage. And so it became, not for its relics, but for its university, and for one professor in particular, Martin Luther. For Luther accelerated the movement to a state church educational system by his discrediting of the magic of Catholic faith. This 'magic' centred round indulgences, which in 1517 were being sold by the agent of the Archbishop of Mainz to repay a loan raised from the Fuggers to purchase his benefice. The agent encountered Luther who 'posted' to his clerical superiors some 95 reasons why he, as a monk, thought such selling of indulgences was wrong. Luther argued that indulgences were based on the idea that sinners could, through priestly intercession, draw on a 'treasury of merit', accumulated by Christ's sacrifice and the good deeds of the saints, and suggested that guilt could be expurgated by faith alone.

From condemning indulgences to attacking the entire ecclesiastical hierarchy was a short step, and when he took it the King of England, Henry VIII, earned the papal accolade of Defender of the Faith for writing against him.

But Henry VIII himself was to collide with the Pope

and Lutheranism became increasingly attractive to him as his negotiations over his divorce petered out. So he turned to Wittenberg where several Englishmen had already been studying with Luther. One of these was Robert Barnes, the puritan, who became a great friend of Luther's barber. So Henry selected him as his envoy to secure German support for his divorce and second marriage.

Barnes was to play an even bigger rôle in the theological debates and changes that followed the divorce, in that with others he brought Lutheranism so much to the forefront in the Thirty-nine Articles of the Anglican Church. A later writer described Anglicans as belonging to 'Martin's Church'—a hybrid between Papist Rome and Calvinist Geneva.

Its propagation: grammar schools and books

The fibre of protestantism was strengthened by learning the 'holy languages'—Latin, Greek and Hebrew. To teach these, 'grammar schools' were founded, in which secularized miracle-plays were encouraged by burghers and schoolmasters. German schools would often lend properties to towns whilst towns often contributed to the cost of such plays.

Because such plays were in Latin, schoolmasters in Germany and England could communicate more easily. English protestants especially admired the *gymnasium* at Strasbourg (sustained by the city), where the school play in both Latin and Greek became a permanent institution (Herford, 1886, 101–6). A tribute to Sturm, the remarkable headmaster of the Strasbourg School was paid by Roger Ascham in *The Schoolmaster* (1570) a book described by its author as 'a rude porch' to Sturm's techniques, which were being practised for eleven years after the book appeared. Some of Sturm's numerous educational writings were also translated into English by a mysterious writer, 'T.B.'.

Several such miracle plays for children were written by

the headmaster of a school at Hitchin, Ralph Radcliffe, whilst the first known English comedy *Ralph Roister Doister* was written by Nicholas Udall, headmaster of Eton.

If Strasbourg was the model grammar school, Frankfurt was the market for books. The first catalogue of new books for sale there was issued in 1564 by George Willer from Augsberg. Here came Bodley's father in the reign of Queen Mary. Bodley himself never lost a passion for books—a passion enhanced by four years spent in Germany, France and Italy as a young man. After joining the Queen's service he was sent abroad in 1585, and from 1589–96 he became the Queen's personal resident in the Netherlands. The following year he devoted himself to restoring the library at Oxford, and sent John Bell to buy books for him abroad. Five years after his death Bell issued the first English version of the Frankfurt Catalogue in 1618.

Its perversion: diabolic science

By the end of the sixteenth century Wittenberg was known not so much as the home of protestantism as the home of magic. If protestantism meant Luther, magic meant Dr. Faustus. Mining and navigation needed mathematics, which was regarded by many as diabolic.

The very suspicion of mathematics led its devotees to conceal its truth in codes. Luther's friend Dürer is said to have concealed a statement of the canon of proportion in his picture *Melancolia*. Certainly Rudolf II the Holy Roman emperor, who patronized scientists like Tycho Brahe, was regarded as mad.

Most English tales of wonder were (or alleged to be) translated out of 'Hie Almain', so much so that it was said that 'the literature of marvels was almost the only direction in which the literary communication between the two countries remained relatively flowing and vigorous' (Herford, 1886, 178).

Here the legend of Dr. Faustus arose. Certainly the magi, whether actual or fiction, seemed to be German: Albertus

3

Magnus Agrippa, Paracelsus, Frethheim. Just such a magus was Faust or Fastus, a legendary character who appeared at this time as the archetype of necromoncer and charlatan. Round him clustered so many legends associated with wizardry that a book was published about him in 1587. Seeing its dramatic possibilities Christopher Marlowe wrote a play on the subject. Marlowe implies that Dr. Faustus was at Wittenberg University, but provided a sop to the Protestant conscience by having his hero cast insults at the Roman Catholic Church.

So if Wittenberg could have a Faustus, so could Oxford. It was supplied by Robert Greene in the same year (1594) as Marlowe's play was performed in *The honorable historie of Friar Bacon and Friar Bungay* (1594). In this, British magicians display their art at the expense of their German counterpart before the German emperor, the King of England and of Castile. When the King of England said 'Now, monarchs, hath the German found his match' (ii, 126), it showed that in magic, as in theology and trade, England was flexing her national muscles against Germany.

Religious peace and the groups

One German merchant who settled in England in 1628, believing that the spread of knowledge would damp the fires of war, started a correspondence with many scholars and men of science and tried to put Comenius (whom he invited to England) at the head of an institution which would effect this—unsuccessful because of the English civil war. Milton dedicated his tract on *Education* (1644) to him, and John Evelyn described him as 'master of innumerable curiosities and very communicative'. This German, Samuel Hartlib, was not alone amongst his countrymen in seeking to alleviate men's needs by knowledge. Another German, Theodore Haak, suggested regular meetings of knowledgeable men, and a group took shape in London in 1645, chiefly at his suggestion (McKie, 1960, 15). When this group developed into the Royal Society of

London, a third German, Henry Oldenburg (the son-in-law of Hartlib's friend John Dury) suggested that it should mount a journal. So not only did he found the *Philosophical Transactions* but for twelve years he edited and published (in spite of being gaoled at one period) it (Bluhm, 1960, 189).

The Royal Society was only one of numerous groups fostered by earnest Germans in England. The preacher at Haak's funeral sermon in 1690 was the Rev. Anthony Horneck who was especially active in forming others. These were not for the improvement of natural knowledge, but for the improvement of civilized manners. Horneck initiated the practice of twice weekly devotional meetings at his house to foster faith, which he had seen at Frankfurt conducted by P. J. Spener in 1666. For Spener intensified the activity of the protestant laity by emphasizing their spiritual priesthood. To him the practical aspect of Christianity was its charity, which deflated controversy. Spener's groups (*collegia pietatis*) of earnest young laymen appealed to Horneck who, on his return to England from the Palatinate in 1671 gathered a *collegium pietatis* around him at the Savoy Chapel. They drew up careful regulations for their conduct.

So began those societies for the reformation of manners. Other clergy like Dr. William Beveridge and Dr. Josiah Woodward followed Horneck's lead in establishing similar groups (Bullock, 1963, 127). Indeed the latter published in 1696 (the year after Horneck's death) *An Account of the Rise and Progress of the Religious Societies in the City of London etc. and of Endeavours for the Reformation of Manners.*

Pietism

Woodward's German translator was one of the foundation professors at the University of Halle: A. H. Francke. Appalled by the ignorance of the poor who came to his house for alms every Thursday, he had started a schools

5

system. It grew rapidly. A boarding establishment (or *Paedagogium*) was organized for sons of the nobility where French, English, Italian and estate-management were taught.

Most interestingly, science, in the form of dissecting dogs or field excursions was cultivated. Similar 'practical subjects' were in the curriculum of a gymnasium he established with the exception that Hebrew took the place of French. The elementary schools he established were similarly oriented to practical ends, like speaking, singing, arts and crafts. Francke's educational practices were down to earth, based on co-operative work. 'Setting' replaced 'classes', music took the place of games, and everyone worked hard. The Paedagogium, for instance, had an eleven hour day (5 to 12, 2 to 6).

Many Englishmen were interested in Francke's work. The founding of Charity schools upon the same plan as that of Halle in Germany was initiated by Francis Lee and Robert Nelson both of whom had travelled through Germany absorbing the pietist spirit of service. Both were also interested in societies for the improvement of manners, and other ameliorative schemes. Both joined the Society for Promoting Christian Knowledge (1695) and Society for the Propagation of the Gospel (1701). Francke's work was further brought to the attention of English readers in *Pietas Hallensis; or a publick demonstration of the footsteps of a Divine Being yet in the world: in an historical narration of the Orphan House and other charitable institutions at Glaucha near Halle in Saxony ... done out of High-Dutch into English* (1705) which Dr. Josiah Woodward commended to the American divines. Yet another disciple was Anthony Boehm, one of the first graduates of the University of Halle, who arrived in England in 1701 to open a school for the children of German families in London. Having met the Prince Consort's secretary on the boat coming over, he was also appointed to read the book of common prayer in the royal chapel. He became the English missionary of the practical Christianity of the Pietists. In

6

The First Principles of Practical Christianity, in Questions and Answers, expressed in the very Words of Scripture (1708) he contributed to the greater understanding of Francke's work. He is thought to have translated *Nicodemus or Treatise Against the Fear of Man* (1706) which was later to be abridged by John Wesley.

Moravians and Wesleyans

Wesley was also influenced by another German, Count Zinzendorf, who had reacted against the joyless eleven hour day of Francke's Paedagogium (after spending six years there) by starting a school of his own near Dresden. Refugees from Bohemia and Moravia built a little settlement on his estate known as Herrnhut and adopted him as leader. So Zinzendorf in return rejected catechetical teachings, and encouraged the singing of hymns, as 'the best method of inculcating religious truths and for conserving those in the heart'. Stripping the Bible of its Jewish accretions, he translated it into modern idiom, taking one such verse as a motto for each day. In pamphlets, 365 at a time, these mottoes (or Kinder-Loosungen) became the theme for activities on that day. Rejecting Francke's emphasis on 'conversion', Zinzendorf tried to reveal Christ to a child 'as clearly as he can see a house': to 'walk' with him. That the child could be free to do so, self-activity was to be encouraged, directed by the Holy Spirit.

This was the real origin of 'progressive' education in a structured environment. This 'structured environment' encompassed old and young, who were organized into 'groups' called 'choirs' by Zinzendorf. Infants, little children, bigger boys, bigger girls, young men, young women, widows, widowers and parents all had their own meetings, litanies and festivals. Socialization was to be the essence of happiness.

Wesley met Moravian missionaries on his way to Georgia. On his return he attended a meeting of the Moravians in Aldersgate Street on 24 May 1738, when he 'felt his heart strangely warmed.' 'I felt,' he wrote 'I did trust in Christ, Christ alone, for salvation; and an assurance was given me, that He had taken away *my* sins, even *more*, and saved *me* from the law of sin and death.' From this time for the next fifty years he was to preach the gospel. In this work frequent hymns on the Moravian pattern as 'a body of experimental and practical divinity' played an essential rôle. He published the first collection of hymns for use in the Church of England, and, aided by his brother Charles, some fifty further tracts and books of hymns followed. Of the 525 hymns in *The Methodist Hymn Book* of 1780 several are translations from the German. Indeed the giving of place names to tunes—Leipzig, Jena, Herrnhut, etc. was begun by him.

Quiet, modest, peaceable, the Moravians went on to become school builders in their settlements in Britain. In addition to Fulneck (their first), girls' schools at Dukinfield and Gomershall (1792), Wyke (1794), Fairfield (1796), Gracehill (1798), Ockbrook (1799) and Bedford (1801) were founded, followed by boys' schools at Fairfield (1801), Gracehill (1805) and Ockbrook (1813). These schools had no competitive games, were open to children of all religions (Catholics included) and produced, in the shape of personalities like Richard Oastler, some very highly motivated alleviators of the miseries of early industrialism.

The Moravian influence on education continued well into the nineteenth century through their school at Neuwied on the Rhine where a number of English boys, including the novelist George Meredith, were educated. One old pupil, Henry Morley, himself established an experimental school in Cheshire (Stewart and McCann, 1967, 289–298).

2

Miners, Merchants, Mercenaries, Missionaries and Musicians

Miners

Wittenberg symbolised the dual image which Germany has presented to England over the last four centuries and a quarter: an image of piety, industry and religious devotion on one side, and a cleverness that seems diabolical on the other. When phased the other images appeared in the shape of ingenious miners, merchants, mercenaries, mechanics and musicians that no doubt enabled Shakespeare to raise a laugh by comparing a woman in *Love's Labour Lost* to:

> a German clock,
> Still arepairing, ever out of frame,
> And never going aright.

For the paper on which Shakespeare wrote might well have been German since Sir John Spielmann had established his famous paper-mill at Dartford in 1588, and the curious can still see the German inscription around his tomb in the local parish church where he was buried in 1626.

Their 'pertinacious industry in manual experiments and their great courage in daring to haunt untrodden paths in the quest of nature's secrets' (Gibb, 1957, 678), was no-where better exhibited than in the activities of their miners who, ever since the Fuggers of Augsberg had formed their company in 1494, had been screwing silver, iron and copper ore out of the hills of Silesia, Hungary, Carinthia, Tyrol and Bohemia.

Since they monopolised lore as well as ore—a lore, which a later German was to call technology—English kings tempted German miners to England. So Edward VI invited Joachim Gundelfinger, Queen Mary invited Bur-chard Kranich, and Queen Elizabeth, Daniel Hoechstetter. As the two great German-led British mining enterprises took shape in 1565 (the Company of Miners Royal and the Mineral and Battery Works), a classic German treatise on metallurgy, the *De re metallica* of the German Agricola (George Bauer) was published.

Of the 136 Germans settled at Keswick under the Mines Royal to mine copper, one travelled to see (and probably advise) Sheffield lead smelters (Donald, 1955, 376). Nor were these the only German craftsmen. Others from Augsberg, Cologne, Innsbruck and Nuremberg had been brought over to introduce the manufacture of fine armour into England. These Almains, as they were called, formed the nucleus of an ambitious scheme to build up Green-wich as an arsenal.

Merchants

'I came from Danzig by land through all the marine towns except Stade and Emden, and found no Englishman trad-ing' wrote Christopher Hoddesdon in 1601. He was looking back to 1544 when English merchants were unknown in Germany. As Queen Elizabeth's financial adviser, and master of the Merchant Adventurers he remedied that de-ficiency and led English merchants into Germany.

Ever since 1267 English needs had been met by a group of German merchants in England trading on the site of what is now the Cannon Street Railway Station, at a post known as the Steelyard. (The name seems to have stemmed from the Middle low German word for sample (stâl), or from the beam on which the samples were weighed. Yet others think that German steel could have been bought there, or perhaps Swedish osmund from which arrow-heads and fish-hooks could be fashioned). Here Englishmen bought the Baltic yew for their bows, Hungarian copper for their weapons and ornaments, Russian furs for warmth, Danzig beer to drink, to say nothing of salt, potash, pitch, amber, grain and honey.

Known as Teutonics of Almain, Pruciers (Prussians), Easterlings or Hansers, these merchants of the Steelyard were the English headquarters of that remarkable confraternity of some sixty or more German cities known as the Hanseatic League that had some forty-five or so 'branches' in England, Wales and Ireland, as well. In these 'branches' the Hanse collected woollens, worsteds and other items, loaned money, and supplied materials of war.

One English king (Edward IV) was virtually restored to his throne by the Hanse, which was so intimately linked with English finance that some people argue that the concept of the pound sterling stems 'from the reliable funding of the Easterlings'. But by Elizabeth's time English merchant venturers like Christopher Hoddesdon were breaking into Germany, Hamburg had long wanted the English factory of the Merchant Venturers and petitioned the Queen in 1564 to this effect. A detachment did arrive and a concord was signed in 1567, but the hostility of the other Hanseatic towns led them to flee to Emden, Middleburg and Stade for a time. Banished from Germany by Imperial decree in 1597, English merchants had made themselves so indispensable in German trade that by 1611 they were back in Hamburg for good. This German staple was to be their stronghold until 1807, when the French armies occupied the town.

Through Hamburg went cloth, lead, tin, leather, corn, beer 'and divers other things' to Germany and out came Rhenish wine, fustians, copper, steel, hemp, linen and gunpowder. Moreover, they raised money on loan for the Queen, manipulated the exchanges to delay the Spanish armada for a year, and, amongst other things, founded scholarships for students at the universities.

After 1688, individual English merchants established themselves in Germany whilst their German counterparts came to England. Thus John Hudson went to Altona in 1737 (the city outside Hamburg) and in six years had 100 looms (Heaton, 1965, 277), whilst John Berkenhaut settled in the West Riding. His son and namesake studied in Germany, entered the Prussian army and transferred to the British army in 1756. Subsequently qualifying in medicine at Edinburgh and Leyden he published a three volume outline of the natural history of Britain. Nor was his rôle as a cultural agent unique. These Germans made enormous contribution not only to the cultural life of the West Riding but to any town in the north of England where they settled.

The responsive commercial networks of English factors, were, said Daniel Defoe, 'not only many in number but some are very considerable in their dealings, and correspond with the farthest provinces in Germany' (Heaton, 1965, 384). Thus English Grammars could be said to be an index of the growth of trade: Aedler's (1680), Offelen's (1686–7), King's (1706) and Beiler's (1731). The really big problem in learning German, however, (the place of words in a sentence), was described in an anonymous *True Guide to the German Language* (1758). German clergymen in London helped, as did English clergymen who had served abroad. And so English merchants prospered by clothing the Hessian and Hanoverian troops.

Mercenaries

German troops fighting alongside the British, also contributed to the spread of the language. During the American War, German officers were said to have 'communicated the knowledge of their books and language'. Pamphlets, plays, novels and other light pieces, were circulated in America, and found their way, after the peace, into England' (Francis Jeffrey, *Edinburgh Review*, January 1804).

Such wars had an important educational by-product: the establishment of an Academy at Woolwich by George II in 1741 'to instruct' the raw and inexperienced people belonging to 'the Military Branch ... in the several parts of Mathematics necessary to qualify them for the Service of the Artillery, and the business of Engineers'. Here was offered 'the first systematic course in mechanical science organized in Britain' (Hamilton, 1958, 351) and to direct it, the mathematician John Müller was brought from Germany. So important did military engineers become that they became a corps of commissioned officers in 1759. As well as training this corps, Woolwich was also responsible for training officers for the Regiment of Artillery which had been created forty-three years earlier. The 'educational realism' (Hogg, 1963, 364) of the Woolwich course led to it being renamed the Royal Military Academy under a Lieut.-Governor, instead of being a part-time chore of the President of the Royal Society. Professors of Fortification and Artillery, of Mathematics and other 'masters' were appointed to teach classics, writing and arithmetic, and by 1766, a lower school was set up to cope with the illiterate.

Cadets were examined by a board under the chairmanship of the President of the Royal Society. But though further staff were appointed for fortification, dancing and French none was appointed for German. Why not? For German was not taken seriously even in Germany. 'Although the German muse is now admired over all Europe', wrote Dr. John Moore in 1779, 'the French language prevails in all the courts and French plays are represented there in preference to German. ... The native language of the country is treated like a vulgar and provincial dialect'. So much so that he met with people 'who considered it as an accomplishment to be unable to express themselves in the language of their country, and who have pretended to be more ignorant in this particular than they were in reality' (Bruford, 1937, 87).

Missionaries

If the German mercenary saved the sum of things for pay, the German missionary did it for love.

In communicating with the people of the vast Indian sub-continent, the East India Company made great use of German missionaries in India, especially the ones chosen by Francke. In the early eighteenth century Schultze became a missionary for S.P.G., translating the Bible into Telego (Gentoo), writing a Hindu grammar and organizing a colloquium for schoolmasters.

After his return to Halle in 1743 he trained other missionaries, notably C. F. Schwarz who stayed in India for fifty years—up till 1798, travelling widely as a negotiator between the Company and the native princes, and trusted by both sides. He even obtained money for his mission from Germany.

> Content with plain living (they) seem to have all things in common among them, one chest sufficing for their common store, and one room to lodge in, and an Arabick or Syriack book is of more value to them than a suit of clothes would be above what they at present want. 'I am afraid,' remarked the Secretary of the S.P.C.K. in 1719, 'we shall never find these qualities in the education of Great Britain.' (Lowther Clarke, 1959, 63).

Nor in the education of Great Britain could be found the restless energy that enabled German clergy in England, like Dr. G. F. Wendelborg, to act as the English correspondent of a Hamburg newspaper, the pastor of a German church at Ludgate Hill, to compile *Elements of German Grammar* (1774), and to learn twelve languages. His *Commercial Dictionary* of 1816 offered 'a clear and concise explanation of every mercantile phrase and technical term'.

Musicians

'One Handel, a foreigner and his lowsey crew of foreign fiddles' visited Oxford in 1713 to perform his oratorio *Athaliah* (Fiedler, 1939, 9). Later, as organist to the Duke of Chandos, George Frederick Handel composed in 1720 music for the masque *Haman and Mordecai*. In 1731 the Bishop of London refused permission for it to be acted, so Handel put it on at the Haymarket Theatre. *Esther*, as it was called, was a prelude to *Deborah* (1732) until he produced *The Messiah* (1742).

Handel's predecessor as organist to the Duke started another fashion by arranging the songs and overture for *The Beggar's Opera*, the first of the Ballad operas. He, too, was a German: Dr. J. C. Pepusch. Another form of musical entertainment—the pantomime—was created by yet another German, J. E. Galliard, whilst light opera was adorned by J. F. Lampe, author of *Plain and Compendious Method of Teaching Thorough-Bass* (1737). Musical instruments introduced into England include the German flute (J. J. Quantz in 1727), the clarinet (by J. C. Bach in 1762 who also popularized the newly invented piano forte) and the oboe (by J. C. Fischer in 1768).

A hautboy in the Hanoverian guards who was sent by his parents in 1757 to England, became an organist at Doncaster, then at Halifax, then at Bath. Turning from harmony to the heavens he became one of the greatest astronomers of his generation, discovering with the help of his sister Lucretia thousands of nebulae and hundreds of stars. This was Sir William Herschell, whose equally gifted son was to help revolutionize the teaching of mathematics at Cambridge early in the nineteenth century.

Handel's challenge to the Italian family of opera and oratorio composers, the brothers Bononcini, was well caught by a contemporary Manchester shorthand teacher, John Byrom:

Some say, that Signor Bononcini
Compared to Handel's a mere ninny,
Others aver, to him, that Handel
Is scarcely fit to hold a candle
Strange! that such high dispute shou'd be
'Twixt Tweedledum and Tweedledee.

3

Allies against Napoleon

Hamburg: safety valve in the blockade

As the German states became allies of Britain in the wars against France, the desire to interpret their works into English increased. J. C. Mellish, British consul in Weimar from 1795 to 1813, did this for both Goethe and Schiller. Goethe stood as godfather to his son, and he rented Schiller's house.

British merchants like Mellish's firm staged bogus funerals with coffins filled with coffee and sugar to the suburbs of Hamburg during the Napoleonic blockade, and returned with corn. For Hamburg became a passive outlet and inlet valve for England into Europe after 1795 (Horn, 1967, 196).

Among others who came to Hamburg were Thomas Campbell (the son of a merchant who had been ruined by the American War and who himself three times seriously considered emigrating to America) where he wrote 'ye mariners of England', later returning to London to edit the *New Monthly Magazine*; Thomas Holcroft (an unsuccessful schoolmaster turned novelist and dramatist) established a journal called *The European Repository*, and Hannibal Lloyd who after his time there returned to England to compose a German-English grammar which long remained the standard work in German universities.

Others went to Bremen, like George Crabb, a Yorkshire schoolmaster. Arriving there in 1806 he supported himself by teaching English. On his return he published a very successful book—*Elements of German and English Conversation on Familiar Subjects*, making available to Englishmen the work of J. C. Adelung, the eighteenth century German lexicographer and philologist.

Professors in the universities began to trade criticisms with each other. The Professor of Greek at Cambridge was attacked by Gottfried Hermann of Leipzig for his *Hecuba* (1797): the Cambridge professor, none other than the redoubtable Richard Porson was very annoyed and circulated a rhyme that has become famous:

> The Germans in Greek
> Are sadly to seek;
> Not five in five score,
> But ninety-five more:
> All; save only HERMAN
> And HERMAN'S a German.
>
> (Clarke, 1937, 69)

'Altertumwissenschaft'

For whilst these professors were quarrelling over metres, Porson's exact German contemporary, F. A. Wolf, was investigating before the world the new science of *Altertumwissenschaft*: the systematic study of archaeology, philosophy, mythology and philology of the ancient world.

Instead of fawning on Napoleon, the Grimms busied themselves with collecting the vanishing myths, folk-lore and stories of their countryside. From an old lady in Kassel they gathered stories like those of Little Red Riding Hood, Snow White and Rose Red, and Hansel and Gretel. The English translation of their stories by Sara Austin's cousin, Edgar Taylor, adorned by the caricaturist, George Cruikshank, set a taste for fairy-tales. The success of Tom

18

Thumb, the Queen Bee, the Frog Prince and Rumpelstilt-
skin led others to raid this copious larder to satisfy a demand which 'seems to have been unsatiable' (Stockley,
1929, 250).

The German belief that truth could be found in the
time-process itself, led to the reading of various books
rather than one. Hitherto truth (or the revelation of eter-
nal being) had not been looked for in human affairs since
they were so impermanent and fluid. But Germans especially began to read 'in order to force from history the ultimate truth it could offer to God-seeking people' (Arendt,
1961, 69).

From the Napoleonic wars was born the system of
study of German history. Stein, architect of resistance to
Napoleon, turned to build up an archive: the Monumenta
Germaniae Historica, in which German writers would be
treated in the same critical spirit as the classics. Without
this, Ranke confessed he 'would never have attracted a
circle of young men to these studies'. And Ranke began,
in 1833, the first seminar to train historical specialists.
To him, the highest aim of the historian was to ascertain
'wie es geschehen ist', i.e. how it came about.

Latching on to the pre-revolutionary ideas of Lessing
that religions were school books of humanity, all of
them relative, historians appealed to history rather than
God to justify men's ways to men. Germans in Germany
became ever more Germanocentric. For side by side with
the view that law and institutions were the expression of
national life (Eichhorn) there developed the notion of
philology as a kind of history of the Teutonic languages.
Even Jacob Grimm, careful and critical scholar as he was
confessed that his works 'derived their strength from the
fatherland'.

Fichte and the fight back

After Prussia had collapsed before Napoleon at the battle
of Jena in 1806 Hegel argued that 'education and intelli-

gence has defeated crude efficiency'. He, like Goethe, had looked to Napoleon as the unifier and pacificator of Europe. The defeat of Jena changed all that.

For after Jena and even more after Auerstadt (1806), and the peace of Tilsit (1807) Prussia needed inspiration not explanation. Such inspiration was forthcoming in the winter of 1807–8 from J. G. Fichte whose *Addresses to the German Nation* hailed the second Luther, to whom 'we must look for our regeneration': J. H. Pestalozzi. The following year, when William von Humboldt became Director of Ecclesiastical Affairs and Public Instruction, the University of Berlin was opened, a qualifying examination for secondary teachers was introduced, a Normal School in Konigsberg was opened and eighteen students sent to Pestalozzi at Yverdun. These teachers trained others, and this advanced guard to Yverdun were the first of many who later returned to open other Normal schools.

Fichte was the apostle of state education:

> *compulsion* itself is education—the education to understanding of moral destiny.... The principle is now quite easy that the State, with all its compulsory measures, must regard itself as an educational institution for making compulsion unnecessary. (Turnbull, 1926, 283, 281)

Though Fichte never carried out his own plan to take into his own house the sons of some of his friends and educate them along with his son, he publicly endorsed Pestalozzi, who had taken into his farm at Neuhof (near Zurich) twenty poor children and, in educating them, evolved the ideas that formed the basis of *Leonard and Gertrude*. As 'the first to point definitely to Pestalozzi, and the first to recognize and state publicly the significance of Pestalozzi's ideas on education for the moral and political regeneration of the State' (Turnbull, 1926, 185) Fichte identified Pestalozzianism with German schools. Young Prussian teachers were sent in regular succession to Yverdun for training in observation, here they were shown how to direct the sense of their pupils to objects and to arouse their consciousness by the impressions so produced.

Secondly, by stressing the emancipating power of the state, Fichte (and von Humboldt and Hegel) inspired English political philosophers like Coleridge and later T. H. Green and Bernard Bosanquet.

The Turners

Impressed by Fichte's *Addresses to the German Nation* Friedrich Jahn, then a young teacher in Berlin, approached him with a scheme for reorganizing student life. As the young teacher saw it they should be as physically fit as a group of gymnasts who from 1811 he was voluntarily training in his spare time in the open spaces outside the city. If other such groups could be encouraged, Jahn thought indeed was determined, to revive what he considered as the old German spirit, by binding young men together by the discipline of fitness (*turnkunst*). These groups would then become the nucleus of a nationalist movement. Just as at Halle the study of philology bred, or led to, Prussian patriotism, so from his mental work with F A. Wolf he was led to write *The Enrichment of the High German Vocabulary* (1806). Friedrich Jahn went on to cultivate the German body with his *Turnplatz* (1811). Gymnastics, as he saw them, should be conducted in the highest spirit of patriotism. So in 1815 he founded the *burschenshaft* of German students at Jena. Believing they were struggling out of the night of slavery through battle to the sun of liberty, its members adopted black, red and gold as their colours. That these were to become the colours of the German empire was not surprising as Jahn kindled belief in the folk of the greater Germany, which would embrace the Low Countries, Denmark, Prussia and Austria with a new capital Teutona, on the Elbe. Education had to forward this Panhuman-Pan-German folkdom.

Jahn's turners were the boy scouts of the new Germany. Whoever opposed them suffered. When a dramatist attacked them he was murdered in 1819. So the government clamped down on them and many of the teachers fled.

Among those who escaped to England was Carl Voelker who had opened the first *Burschenschaft* and *Turnplatz* at the University of Tübingen. With the help of Jeremy Bentham he opened a *Turnplatz* at 1 Union Place, New Road, near Regent's Park and so successful was he that he opened a supplemental gymnasium in Worship Street, Finsbury Square.

German influence on English literature

As the satanic mills of the Industrial Revolution began to rise to supply the allies, a taste for 'Gothic' fiction developed. This genre owed much to a German schoolmaster, J. K. A. Musaeus, whose collections of German popular tales were translated into English in 1790. Six years later as Jane Austen began in *Northanger Abbey* to satirise these Gothic tales by contrasting them to life as it really was, she described two of them as German. Just how German they were can be seen from *The Monk* (1796), a story written in Germany by M. G. Lewis.

Now too the practice of sending boys to Germany for language training began to be effective. Such a school was set up by L. H. Pfeil, Goethe's father's secretary. Amongst his 'guests' was Arthur Lupton of Leeds who was to become a friend of Goethe himself (Wilkie, 1955, 29). Another practice was to send boys to a German 'pastor'. One such English merchant's son who was sent to Detmold in 1782 at the age of seventeen years was William Taylor who went on to become, after his return to Norwich, almost German in his devotion to business and culture. For his literary labours were astonishing. As translator (Bürger's *Leonore* into English ballad metre, Lessing's *Nathan*, Goethe's *Iphigenia*), critic (he wrote numerous articles for most of the literary reviews), encourager of others (amongst them Southey and that superb literary vagrant George Borrow), he was an agreeable, aggressive distributor of German ideas for over forty years, and deserved a greater praise from Goethe for his *Historic Survey of German Poetry* (1828–30).

The great historical fabulist Sir Walter Scott formed a group in 1792 to learn German. Their teacher was A. F. M. Willich, a pupil of Kant. Under him the group developed an enthusiasm for German stories and ballads. Two years later the group were electrified by a translation of Bürger's ballad *Leonore* when read by Mrs. Barbauld.

Walking in Wales in 1802 seventeen year old Thomas de Quincey met a German dipping into a little portable trunk of books. Once aroused, his interest was yet further kindled at Oxford.

A special periodical had been started in 1800 to cater for those interested in Germany, known as *The German Museum or Monthly Repository of the literature of Germany, the North and the Continent in General.* But it only lasted for three years. When the war was over, two more successful ones appeared : *Blackwood's Magazine* (1815) and *The Westminster Gazette* (1819).

Muscular Christianity

It was from an 1819 exile—Francis Lieber (a former tutor in the family of Niebuhr, the German historian), that Thomas Arnold, then a curate at Laleham, became aware of the gymnastics of Jahn, professing himself 'very much pleased with the pamphlet of Dr. Lieber about Education', and thinking him 'the more worthy of having had so much intercourse with Niebuhr'. Indeed, even after he became headmaster of Rugby he would swing on his 'gallows' (a device used at Yverdun), and gloat

I could laugh like Democritus himself at the notion of my being thought a dangerous person, when I hang happily upon my gallows, or make it serve as a target to spear at.

'Spearing', in fact, was one of his favourite exercises: 'I spear daily', he told someone else in the same year 'as the Lydians used to play in the famine, that I may at least steal some portion of the day from thought'.

It is this entire relaxation, I think, at intervals, [he wrote] that gives me so keen an appetite for my work at other times, and has enabled me to go through it not only with no fatigue, but with a sense of absolute pleasure.

Bathing, cricketing, gardening, Arnold constantly reiterated that daily exercise was essential:

I must have my hour or two of thorough relaxation if I am to do my work [he wrote]. I could not get on as some men do merely with a change of employment. Walking from cottage to cottage in a parish would not be enough for me. I must throw off my work altogether. I must have my playtime. . . . If I am deterred from this my appetite fails me, and then all is over with me. I am good for nothing.

Through him the 'gospel of fitness' spread to the provinces. One of his pupils, C. P. Melly, established in 1858 at his own cost, the first gymnasium for the working classes of Liverpool, and pioneered in the provision of playgrounds for poor children.

Arnold's gospel was given a twentieth century interpretation by another German émigré, Kurt Hahn.

The German 'will to power' in English public life

Arnold's 'disciples', men like Walrond, Clough and Stanley, transmitted his muscular 'geist' to others in turn. This was but only one Germain strain in English public life, generalized by the Napoleonic wars. Another showed in the activities of Lord Milner's 'kindergarten', the 'appeasers' of the 1930's.

For Lord Milner's grandfather James had settled in Germany in 1805, whilst his father was a lecturer at Tübingen. Lord Milner himself was born in Giessen and went to the gymnasium at Tübingen. In England after 1869 for his university education, he decided never to marry so that he could devote himself entirely to the state. In South Africa and later on the Western Front (where he pressed for unity) he was a leader. Though denounced as pro-German he persevered in his efforts to secure a negotiated peace in the First World War to prevent the British and German junker class from going the way of the Russians after 1917. In this, he had the support of yet another German trained British statesman, Lord Haldane.

4

Göttingen to Gower Street
The German University Model

'Wissenschaftlehre'

'Is this "Wissenschaftlehre" Theory of Knowledge by Fichte really a new science as they pretend' asked a young Englishman in 1801. He noted the reply: 'Nothing but *Idealismus*'. So, on the proceeds of an inherited annuity, Crabb Robinson trained himself to become an early advocate of *wissenschaft* (knowledge with an objective flavour) in England in the first quarter of the nineteenth century.

After attending some public lectures on medicine and mathematics at Göttingen in June 1801 (and understanding 'little of the former and nothing of the latter') he wrote to his brother that German universities 'deserve the name of Universities much better than the English Colleges as all the practical Sciences are introduced'. They were 'less immoral', cheaper and more professional, 'mere places of Assembly' rather than 'a sort of School for grown Gentlemen'. He described them as

> places . . . where Professors are nominated to give Lectures on *all the Sciences and branches of Learning*. They have very few public buildings. And often no point of corporate Union. They have no prayers, no Costume, no *obligation* to attend Lectures, no Tests,

few Examins, and only those when Degrees are con-
fered. (Batho, 1929, 74)

At Jena, Crabb Robinson saw no reason to alter the
opinion he formed at Göttingen, and told his brother

> You must dismiss however all Ideas of Monastick Re-
> straint, of discipline, of secret correspondence between
> the learned establishments & the civil government,
> & of a number of other practical absurdities which
> reign in our Academies. The protestant German Uni-
> versities in general are nothing but places of Union
> for Men of Letters & Students, with more or less ad-
> vantages of public Libraries. (Batho, 1929, 114–5)

Göttingen as exponent

Crabb Robinson was not the first to make known the
excellences of Göttingen : a university which had of course
been founded in 1737 by the English King George II as
elector of Hanover.

Any eighteenth-century Englishman on the grand tour
(after George II had founded the University of Göttingen) took it in, for it was 'the most efficient university in
Germany and probably in Europe' (Mare and Quarrell,
1938, x). It had 'the only really satisfactory university
library in Germany, together with scientific and medical
laboratories and museums' (Bruford, 1935). It had
organized a special seminar for teachers, which had been
followed by most of the other German universities. Thus
at Konigsberg, where Kant ran the teachers' seminar
from 1776 to 1777 and from 1786 to 1788, it was held
that

> It is possible for education to become better and better,
> and for each successive generation to take a step nearer
> the perfection of humanity; for behind education lurks
> the great secret for the perfection of humanity. (Buchner,
> 1908, 109)

Perfectibilism intensified motivation. Kant found it so

27

'enrapturing to fancy that human nature will be better and better developed through education', that he drafted routes to the heavenly city of the eighteenth-century philosophers.

One English peer was amazed 'that the Germans invented so many things which the English could not imitate'. Instancing electricity and the medicinal properties of hemlock, the peer 'could scarcely find words to describe what wretched people English artificers generally were in matters of theory' (Mare and Quarrell, 1938, 49). The peer, Lord Polworth, was talking to Lichtenberg, Gottingen's professor of physics in 1780. For science and technology were extensively cultivated at Göttingen. As a background book J. J. Beckman's *History of Inventions and Discoveries* (1779) was later to be translated into English by Wiliam Johnson in 1797. Göttingen's professor of physics was well known in England. J. R. Forster, the traveller who settled in England, was a friend of his. So was Salgasse, tutor to the Prince of Wales, whom he found to be:

> ... the only savant, of all those with whom I have hitherto conversed on this island, who has a fairly precise knowledge of our literature; he reads German and takes particular pleasure in the Göttingen journals, which the Queen regularly communicates to him (Mare and Quarrell, 1938, 82).

In 1799 the University of Göttingen was also visited by Samuel Taylor Coleridge who talked incessantly in the intervals of attending lectures, and gave the impression that his mind was much more German than English. Others who felt the stimulus of Göttingen were Robert Jardine, who later taught German to Thomas Carlyle in 1819 in return for lessons in French (Carlyle, 1886, 209, 227), and John Stuart Blackie who became the first professor of humanity at Aberdeen.

Göttingen-trained scientists were active in early nineteenth-century England too. The growing mining industry had good cause to be thankful to Dr. Konig for building up a collection of mineralogical specimens that were of immense help to his fellow geologists—who also formed themselves into a Society under the presidency of G. B. Greenough. The need to provide adequately qualified medical practitioners for the mushrooming cities led W. T. Brande to play a leading rôle in securing the Apothecaries Act of 1815, which by imposing a qualifying examination on all intending medical practitioners, initiated a whole chain of events to provide postulant apothecaries with the necessary training. From this act stems the establishment of provincial medical schools in England, which either developed into or became part of what are now the civic universities. Other Göttingen trained medical men, like Charles Parry of the Bath General Hospital or J. H. Green, the professor of anatomy to the Royal College of Surgeons were further witnesses to the Göttingen influence in the field of general medicine.

A lecturer in one such medical school in London, Dr. George Birkbeck, played a leading rôle in establishing a University of London in 1827 which should 'combine various points in the German method, with whatever appeared more eligible in the systems pursued at home'.

This adulation of Germany could be taken too seriously, and Sir Walter Scott's friend George Canning sang:

> Whene'er with haggard eyes I view
> This Dungeon, that I'm rotting in
> I think of those Companions true
> Who studied with me at the U-
> —NIVERSITY OF GOTTINGEN,—
> —NIVERSITY OF GOTTINGEN.

Hodgskin and the 'Quiet Insurrection'

As the most lavishly endowed of all the German universities—its revenue was little more than £11,000 p.a., or the income of four college heads in England, Göttingen stood out to English observers as a shining exemplar of the virtues on non-collegiate life. Göttingen has no good things to bribe its younger members to a continued adherence to taught opinion,' wrote Thomas Hodgskin in 1820. 'There is no warm and well-lined stall of orthodoxy, and no means are taken to influence the student's conscience through their stomachs.'

Armed with a questionnaire drafted by Bentham, which is now in the British Museum (Add. MSS, 35, 153, f3ff), he began in July 1818 a systematic examination of the government, religion, trade and agriculture of Germany. Published two years later as *Travels in the North of Germany describing the present state of the Social and Political Institutions of that Country, particularly in the Kingdom of Hanover* (1820), it sharpened the whole tone of the argument of the English reformers. For though Hodgskin deplored state action in education, he found German universities preferable to their English counterparts, even though they were subject to the capricious directions of the sovereign and his ministers (1820, ii, p. 266–7).

Having met and married a German wife he tried to make a living by writing articles for the reviews and teaching German. He even contemplated translating a history of the Hanseatic League. In none of these did he succeed. But after he had been appointed to the staff of a London newspaper he started *The Mechanics' Magazine* to provide readers with:

Accounts of all new Discoveries, Inventions and Improvements, with illustrative Drawings, Explanations of Secret Processes, Economical Receipts, Practical Application of Mineralogy and Chemistry, Plans and Suggestions for the Abridgement of Labour, Reports of the State of the Arts in this and other Countries.

Here the German gospel of technology was to be popularized and Beckman came into his own. By 11 October,

1823, he and Robertson launched an appeal for his mechanic readers to do what the state was doing in Austria and France and form their own educational institutions—not to let the State do it for them. His suggestion was seized upon by Francis Place who amended it by securing help from a corps of wealthy radicals.

Having seen the 'Holy Alliance' at work putting down ideas in Germany, Hodgskin wanted to encourage in England 'the quiet insurrection by which knowledge will subvert whatever is not founded in justice and truth' (Halévy, 1956, 90). So he joined forces with Dr. Birkbeck to lecture in the London Mechanics' Institute on the philosophy of history and on psychology.

Thomas Campbell and London University

The mainly Scots group behind Hodgskin's idea for the London Mechanics' Institute were also much impressed by the argument of Thomas Campbell that a University of London should be founded on the lines of the new universities of Berlin, founded in 1810, and Bonn, founded in 1818. Campbell was especially impressed by the fact that he met Englishmen studying medicine abroad: William Coulson, who later left one of the largest fortunes yet made in medicine, and his fellow Cornishman, E. J. Spry, both of whom had gone to Berlin to study. So, too, the young poet Thomas Lovell Beddoes went to Göttingen in 1825.

Campbell wished to entrust the education of his son (a manic-depressive) to a Bonn professor whose wife was an Englishwoman. On visiting Bonn he was much impressed by its building, the former palace of the electoral prince, the library where he worked, and the people. There was a 'republican equality among the bourgeoisie' whilst even labourers 'have bread to eat and are well paid and employed; I wish our own country could say the same' (Beattie, 1850, 369).

When London University got under way a minor

canon of St. Paul's knew where to aim his satire—with its echo of Canning—*Stinkomalee Triumphans:*

> What precious fools 'the People' grew,
> Their *Alma Mater* not in town—
> The 'useful classes' hardly knew
> Four was composed of two and two,
> Until they learned it at the U-
>   niversity we've Got-in-town.

Not only was it like Göttingen, but like Bonn—a 'lecture-bazaar':

It might even have seemed that there would be a state of affairs described by an admiring scribe of the University of Bonn, where such was the laborious industry and perseverance of the professors that, with some partial intermission, they lectured incessantly, either in public or in private, from seven in the morning until eight in the evening. (Hale Bellot, 1929, 79–80).

Certainly London had a chair of German from the very beginning and its occupant none other than Schliermacher's brother-in-law, Ludwig von Muhlenfels, a refugee from the persecutions of 1819 when he kept open house for members of the German colony in London. Another German held the chair of oriental languages, and later of Sanskrit—F. A. Rosen, whilst a third held the chair of Hebrew. There might have been two more in the chairs of physiology and history respectively, but both refused.

Certainly one of the most influential backers I. L. Goldsmid (later to become the first Jewish baronet) went to Germany to clear their ideas about the new institution and its rôle, and the curious can see in the British Museum (Add. MSS 27, 834, f 301) Goldsmid's impressions of what he found there.

German undenominational professorial-type universities so favourably impressed Samuel Fletcher, a Sunday school teacher of Manchester, that he told George Faulkner, the friend, business partner and intended heir of John Owens, about them. As a result, Faulkner suggested that Owens, instead of making him his heir, should use the money to found an undenominational university college (Thompson, 1886, 96–7). And so Owens College opened its doors in 1851 with Faulkner as the first chairman of trustees.

The Royal Commissions on Oxford and Cambridge

Another Mancunian, the unitarian, James Heywood, had been long campaigning against the religious tests imposed by Oxford and Cambridge. So, he enlisted Francis Newman (unitarian brother of the more famous Roman Catholic convert) who translated V. A. Hüber's *Die Englischen Universitäten* (1839). Another of Heywood's researchers was W. C. Perry, a historian who made a living by taking private pupils at Bonn (amongst them Lord Lytton, Sir Francis Bertie, and Sir Eric Barrington), who helped him add to the second edition an account of the German public schools. Ironically enough, Perry was later prosecuted by the German government for protesting against the abuse levelled against England by the German press (*The Times*, 1 Jan. 1912, P. 11 col. d).

The message was taken inside Oxford and Cambridge. After going to Germany in 1844 and 1845, Benjamin Jowett became convinced that Oxford's 'only defence against attacks from without' was 'to build up from within' and he began to move for an examination system; lay professors, and a more rational examinations system. But other dons feared that 'German Ocean' would drown them, and after the Royal Commission on Oxford and Cambridge had been appointed in 1850, Henry L. Mansel mocked the model that the commissioners were so obviously working towards:

> Professors we
> From over the sea

> From the land where Professors in plenty be;
> And we thrive and flourish, as well we may,
> In the land that produced one Kant with a K,
> And many Cants with a C.

He might have added—and students—for within another ten years Germany had six times as many students per head of population as did Britain (Sparrow, 1967, p. 113).

Giessen and the Gospel of Chemistry

Ironically in the claim for state patronage, professors played one country off against another. Citing the inability of the Prussian student (as compared to his English or French counterpart) to pay his expenses in such few chemical laboratories as there were in Germany, Justus von Liebig protested against having to teach chemistry in the wing of an old barracks. He attacked what he called the 'overgrown humanism' which 'stands above all else against the progress of natural science and scientific medicine', prophesying that it would be 'a thing that will be looked back half a century hence with shame and a smile of pity' (Smithells, 1921, 96).

Like a drill sergeant Liebig tested his faithful band every week in the then novel subject of organic chemistry, reacting with them as effectively as any agent. From their work came chloroform, chloral and methaldehyde. As with most great teachers his ideas were carried abroad. Certainly no disciple of his was more notable in England than the son of the man who gave him his new laboratory soon after the tirade cited above: August Wilhelm von Hofmann.

Just after obtaining his new lab, Liebig visited England. His host was the British Association, to which he lectured on the application of chemistry to agriculture. He was consulted by the Prime Minister, squired by Lyon Playfair, fêted in London and generally treated like a visiting prince of chemists, which indeed he was. One of his English pupils considered him to be 'a Pope believed to be not only infallible, but beyond the reach of question or criticism by any mere mortal" (Haber, 1958, 67). Thanks to him coal tar was split into its constituents, providing scents, solvents, naphtha, dyes, benzole and toluene—the list is endless. These stimulated the demand for more chemists, which, since Britain had not trained enough, were German immigrants like Heinrich Caro, and Carl Alexander Martius (who worked in Manchester). As late as 1883 Levinstein, a Lancashire manufacturer was hoping we could 'turn out at our universities and colleges not more testers, but chemists with a superior knowledge of hydrocarbon derivatives and especially of the coal tar colours.'

Two 'outstations' of Giessen took shape: the Rothamsted Experimental Station in 1843 and the Royal College of Chemistry in 1845. On the headship of the latter he was consulted and recommended Hofmann. The Prince Consort actually met Hofmann at Brühl on the Rhine and personally interceded with the King of Prussia to second him to the school by giving him leave of absence from the University of Bonn for two years. Hofmann stayed not for two years but twelve and as the Prince Consort told the King of Prussia in 1847 raised 'the new Institution to a high pitch of usefulness and popularity' (Linstead, 1962, 21).

During his twelve year stint in London, teaching, the Royal College of Chemistry was merged with a new School of Mines in 1853, becoming in 1862, the year before Hofmann left, the Royal School of Mines.

A third English Giessen, if a minor one, was founded by a pupil of Hofmann's, Sheridan Muspratt: the privately financed Liverpool Chemical College, opened in 1848. Later Peter Griess established a laboratory in, of all places, the Burton brewers, Allsop and Sons.

German yeast: Prince Albert

Beer was not the only national product that was improved by German skills. The most active German reagent in England from 1840 to 1859 was Prince Albert. As a successful husband, he deplored the great divorce taking place in England between education and industry and as a self-appointed marriage guidance counsellor, did his best to prevent it by staging a festival of their nuptials: the Great Exhibition of 1851.

His idea was to use the profits of this exhibition to found four schools of science and industry at South Kensington. He also hoped to concentrate all the scientific societies here, together with the Institution of Civil Engineers in a Napoleonic-type technical-national university. But costs and inertia were against him, and instead, Departments of Science and Art were founded with his two associates Lyon Playfair and Henry Cole as secretaries.

The Department of Science and Art (as it was known after 1856), played its part, however. It was the first opening through which state aid could be profitably given to scientific instruction. As a kind of precursor of the Department of Education and Science its operations expanded as a result of the events outlined in Chapter 7.

As the tactless Bertie Stanhope blurts out at the Bishop of Barchester's party in Chapter XI of *Barchester Towers* (1857):

'Talking of professors, how much you Englishmen might learn from Germany; only you are too proud.'
'German professors!' groaned out the chancellor, as though his nervous system had received a shock which nothing but a week of Oxford air could cure.
'Yes,' continued Ethelbert; ... 'You'll have those universities of yours about your ears soon, if you don't consent to take a lesson from Germany.' (Chap. xi)

Nor was it only the higher ecclesiastics who thought

like this. Brianite evangelists could denounce curates who preached sanitation before sanctity as protection against the cholera. Charles Kingsley's curate in *Two Years Ago* (1857) found himself denounced ... in chapel (on) Sunday as a German rationalist, who 'impiously pretended to explain away the Lord's visitation into a carnal matter of drains, and pipes, and gases, and such like.' The intransigent Oxford controversialist Dr. Tatham expressed the heartfelt sentiments of most conservative Englishmen when, in the pulpit, he most heartily wished 'all the Jarman critics at the bottom of the *Jarman ocean*' (Cox, 1870, 233–4).

Let us now look at the work of some of these critics and see why Dr. Tatham disliked them.

5

The 'ologies

Geology versus Genesis

Theologians we,
Deep thinkers and free
From the land of the new Divinity;
Where critics hunt for the sense sublime,
Hidden in texts of the olden time
Which none but the sage can see.
Where Strauss shall teach you how Martyrs died
For a moral idea personified,
A myth and a symbol, which vulgar sense
Received for historic evidence
Where Bauer can prove that true Theology
Is special and general Anthropology
And the essence of worship is only to find
The realized God in the human mind.
Where Feuerbach shows how Religion began
From the deified feelings and wants of man,
And the Deity owned by the mind reflective,
Is Human Consciousness made objective
Presbyters, bend,
  Bishops attend;
The Bible's a myth from beginning to end.

So Mansel summed up the impact on religion of the sciences.

Geology, defined by Dr. Johnson in his *Dictionary* (1755) as 'the doctrine of the earth' had been not so much taught as preached in the School of Mines at Freiberg by A. G. Werner. From 1775 till his death in 1817 he exhorted his students to believe that the distribution of minerals over the globe affected the migrations and characters of people, the arts of life, indeed the destiny of civilization. Such mineralogical determinism proved highly popular, and was preached at Edinburgh by his disciple, Robert Jameson, who as Regius Professor of natural history, established a Wernerian Society there in 1805.

Jameson's friend, Sir David Brewster, also knew a German 'unifier' of the natural sciences, Lorenz Oken. Oken flirted with ideas of the cellular structure of organisms, and organized—at Jena in 1822—a 'Parliament of scientists'. This met annually, and was attended by the British mathematician Charles Babbage in 1828, the British botanist Robert Brown in 1829 and the British chemist, J. F. W. Johnstone in 1830. Anxious to see it emulated in England, the last named asked, in the *Edinburgh Journal of Science* (N.S., iv, 1831), whether a similar institution could not be founded in England.

His question obtained an affirmative and effective reply from the editor, Sir David Brewster, who wrote to the secretary of the Yorkshire Philosophical Society suggesting York as a centre for the first meeting of an English counterpart. This duly took place in September 1831. So the British Association took shape as a resonant amplifier of British scientists' gospel of 'emulating the Germans'.

Geology was yet further strengthened a year later when the geological survey was set up by the Government. Its director, Henry de la Beche, had begun a geological map at his own expense until in 1832 the government appointed him to direct the geological survey. Twenty years later on the site of the present shop of Messrs. Simpson, between Jermyn Street and Piccadilly, was set up what became the Royal School of Mines. This was de la Beche's brainchild. He envisaged it becoming a general school of applied science.

Opened on 12 May 1851 by the Prince Consort as the Government School of Mines and of Science applied to the Arts, it marked, in the words of its mid-twentieth-century director 'a milestone in British educational history because it was a *Government* school, and in supporting it the Government was for the first time investing money directly in higher scientific education' (Linstead, 1862, 24).

Foundations of faith

Just as the undermining of the earth's crust was facilitated by the skills spread by German geologists, so the superstructure of faith was being eroded by the activities of German theologians. Like termites they attacked the Bible. The first application of rigorous historical and linguistic techniques to the Old Testament was made by J. G. Eichorn at Jena and Göttingen. His influence rippled out beyond the immediate circle of biblical critics to affect writers like Herder. Later the first effective application of such techniques to the New Testament was made at Tubingen by F. C. Baur, who showed how early Christianity was the outcome of a conflict between primitive Jewish messianism and Gentile reactions, resulting in the so-called Pauline epistles having to be written in the second century to reconcile the two. From this sweeping post-dating of the epistles he excepted those to the Corinthians, the Galatians and the Romans. According to Baur this conflict can be seen in the gospels whose authors were really adaptors or redactors of earlier gospels.

Baur, and his even more fearsome namesake, Bruno Bauer, whose destructive criticism cost him his licence in 1842, epitomized the application, by German biblical scholars, of the full range of historical techniques and philosophical insights to the New Testament, an application perhaps best seen in D. F. Strauss *Das Leben Jesu* (1835) which virtually exploded in the faces of English academics.

At Rugby, Dr. Arnold was horrified, and wrote to his great German friend, Chevalier Bunsen:

> What a strange work Strauss' *Leben Jesu* appears to me, judging of it from the notices in the *Studien und Kritiken*. It seems to me to show the ill effects of that division of labour which prevails so much among the learned men of Germany. Strauss writes about history and myths, but having heard that some pretended histories are mythical, he borrows this notion as an engine to help him out of Christianity. (Stanley, 1890, p. 291)

'Arnold was German, his ideas were that of true religious Germanism' (Brilioth, 1925, 87). He confessed that he owed to them his ability to believe in Christianity 'with a much more implicit and intelligent faith than I otherwise should have been able to have done' (Hocker, 1951, 131).

Thomas Arnold

Arnold was the first Englishman to draw attention in our public schools to the historical, political, and philosophical value of philology and of the ancient writers, as distinguished from the mere verbal criticism and elegant scholarship of the previous century (Stanley, 1890, 78). To him every study required 'to be tempered and balanced with something out of itself, if it be only to prevent the mind from becoming "einseitig" or pedantic' (Stanley, 1890, 289).

As an insurance against atheism, Arnold looked to 'the new creations of our knowledge', gathering themselves 'into a fair and harmonious system, ever revolving in their brightness around their proper centre, the throne of God'. This, with 'prayers and kindly intercourse with the poor' was Arnold's recipe for education.

He hoped for much from Prussia: 'the mountain of the Lord, the City of God upon a Hill whose light cannot be hid' (Stanley, 1890, 392). So he would rather teach boys German than French: 'I am sure,' he told his chairman, 'that there we do facilitate a boy's after-study of the language considerably, and enable him, with much less trouble, to read those many German books, which are so essential to his classical studies at the university' (Stanley, 1890, 79).

The illusion that a historical education could effectively eradicate unpleasant principles was an old one. It animated the creation of the Regius chairs of history at Oxford and Cambridge in 1724, in the hope that 'Tory' principles would be eradicated, and it was certainly the hope of Dr. Arnold at Rugby.

Arnold's friendship with Christian Bunsen was 'all but idolatry' (Stanley, 1890, 211). Bunsen even sent his son Henry to Rugby. 'We are the last reserve of the world' Arnold told Bunsen, 'its fate is in our hands. God's work on earth will be left undone unless we do it' (Gooch, 1913, 320). And God's work was symbolized in a scheme for an Anglo-Prussian bishopric in Jerusalem, as an experiment in what he hoped the Church of England would be: a comprehensive church, embracing people of different liturgies and creeds.

Alas, for human hopes. Arnold died in the very year (1842) Bunsen began his twelve year ambassadorship to England, twelve years in which he sedulously diffused, in dinner parties and amongst his numerous English academic friends the idea of God in History. The Anglo-Prussian bishopric in Jerusalem which he had so patiently negotiated in 1841 was duly established, and the bishop was duly appointed by Prussia and Britain alternately. But the Act of Parliament in 1841 which exempted the incumbent from taking the oath of allegiance also excluded clergy ordained by him from officiating in England and Ireland. The High Church party in England were also very much against it and insisted that the bishop subscribe to the Thirty-nine Articles and be consecrated according to the English rite. The Germans objected to this in turn and so the German emperor finally abolished the agreement in 1886.

Philology

Sent by his tutor, Thirlwall, to Chevalier Bunsen in 1831, Richard Monckton Milnes remained a close friend thereafter. After 1841 when Bunsen was the Prussian ambassador in London, Milnes was a constant visitor, and when Bunsen retired to Heidelberg in 1854, would regularly visit him there. Having studied at the University of Bonn, Milnes was a prominent Germanophile, supporting the 'quiet inoffensive Germans in Germany, who never thought of touching a hair of a Frenchman's head' (Pope-Hennessy, 1951, 230), but the stories told by the numerous French refugees from the siege of Paris led him to castigate it as 'not only wrong but unnecessary'.

Milnes' tutor, Connop Thirlwall, was very much seized of the view that history, ethnology and theology based on classical scholarship encompassing philosophy and mythology was the real field of study, and had started in 1831, with the help of Julius Hare, *The Philological Museum*.

This was virtually a parish magazine for the Germanists, as Julius Hare's passion for things German, stimulated as a boy at Weimar, resulted in him amassing the finest collection of German books in England. Over the years from 1822 to 1832, his passionate and stimulating lectures at Cambridge had started similar trains of thought in his hearers, one of whom, John Sterling, became his curate when he went to the family living at Hurstmonceaux.

No one can read the story of the education of his nephew, Augustus, without realizing how cruel Julius

Hare could be to children. Whipped from the age of five with a riding crop, dosed with rhubarb and senna to condition him against carnal indulgence, locked in the vestry of the church between services, his favourite cat hung: all this pseudo-Spartan upbringing left Augustus so weak that he went to Harrow wearing a kind of harness which saved him from 'things which never could be mentioned but which were of a nightly occurrence all over the School' (Mitford, 1942, 325).

Thirlwall's own Germanophilia led to him leaving Trinity under a cloud. He argued that since Cambridge colleges were neither theological seminaries nor schools of religious instruction, compulsory chapel was an anomaly. Mill regarded him as best speaker he had heard (*Autobiography*, 1873, 125).

Academic history

Arnold's great-nephew, Adolphus William Ward, son of Consul-General at Leipzig from 1845 to 1860, caught the same German fever whilst at school in Leipzig. So much so indeed, that at Cambridge he was said to 'look like a German corps-student'.

Appointed to the chair of History and English Language and Literature at Owens College, Manchester in 1866, Adolphus Ward turned his attention to converting it to a research-type German university. He was one of four professors who issued a pamphlet in 1875 arguing that it become an independent degree-giving university: a case ratified in 1880. Meanwhile he was actively forwarding his enthusiasms at Cambridge. His *Suggestions towards the Establishment of a History Tripos* (1872) was the overture to massive efforts for those great Cambridge co-operative histories which squat on every library shelf like German dolmens, pregnant with erudition. In spite of all this his great ambition remained unfulfilled. It was to write the history of the Hanseatic League.

That these dolmens were raised at all was due to J. E. E.

Dalberg (later Lord) Acton. Son of a German mother and step-son of a Whig Granville, he spent eight years as a pupil of the great Catholic historian Döllinger at Munich, acquiring a passion for books and annotation that was to overpower his creativity. Characteristic of his intellectual debts is the title of his contribution to the first number of the *English Historical Review:* 'The German Schools of History'! Elected to the Regius chair of history at Cambridge he was asked by the University Press to edit a co-operative history. Planned with care, it had to be finished by others on a far less coherent plan than he had envisaged.

Bunsen's protégés

The incarnate philologue was Bunsen's protégé, Max Müller. A German polymath whose knowledge of Sanskrit was such that the East India Company commissioned him to bring out an edition of the Rigveda, he settled in Oxford in 1848. He would have devoted himself to Sanskrit but for the fact that he was defeated in the election for the chair. So he turned to the study of philology, mythology and and comparative religion. The Sacred Books of the East, published under his editorship, gave Englishmen for the first time an opportunity of matching their religion against the largest backdrop yet available. Müller also brought his schoolfellow Victor Carus, the biologist, to Oxford as H. W. Acland's assistant at Christ Church.

Another of Bunsen's protégés was Friedrich Althaus. Sent by Alexander von Humboldt in 1853, he was a schoolmaster, cataloguer and professor—first at the R.M.A. Woolwich, then at University College, London—from 1874 to 1897. He was a friend of Carlyle, and is credited with persuading him to write to support the Prussians in the Franco-German war of 1870.

As a kind of psychiatrist to the disturbed derelicts of the Oxford movement Bunsen was superb. He tried and succeeded in converting the young James Anthony Froude from the shallow atheism that had led him to write *The Nemesis of Faith* and turned his attention to becoming the historian of the great age of British imperialism, whilst he persuaded the unloved and desiccated Mark Pattison to study J. J. Scaliger, and so become a leading disciple of German-type research in British universities. Indeed Pattison's outlook has won, in our own time, sympathetic treatment from V. H. H. Green (1957) and John Sparrow (1967).

The gospel of Geist

Though Victorian England's educational guru, Matthew Arnold, felt 'rather angry to be affiliated to German Biblical critics' he nevertheless confessed that he had 'had to read masses of them'. 'They would have drowned me' he continued 'had it not been for the corks I had brought from the study of Spinoza' (Super, vi, 1968, 455). For, even more than his father Thomas, Matthew Arnold mediated their ideas to the schools, only in his case to the state schools. He urged the Philistines, Barbarians and Populace of Victorian England to 'get Geist' and 'trust to *Ernst der ins Ganze geht*, to mind and not to clap-trap'. The only way to ensure it was, in Arnold's view, 'to put education as a bar, or condition', between every man and what he aims at. This meant compulsory education. To the attainment of this we must now turn.

6

The fight for compulsory education

The Vox Germanica: *Thomas Carlyle*

Studies in mineralogy in which he took 'a transient interest' (Cazamian, 1932, 32) induced the young Scotsman Thomas Carlyle to learn German. This opened a new heaven as well as a new earth to him. For in the German transcendental negation of materialism, and in their love of work, a congenial field opened for his own restless energy.

Over fifty years later he was to tell students of the University of Edinburgh that 'Maid servants, I hear people complaining, are getting instructed in the 'ologies' (Carlyle, 1869, iii, 575). Of all those 'ologies he found the most rewarding to be the secular theology of history. To him, as to the inhabitants of the barren North German plain, it offered routes and roots. But routes to the future, like roots to the past, needed rigorous study, 'the transcendent capacity for taking trouble' which he called genius (Carlyle, 1885, iv, 3).

Discussions of the meaning of history really began with Herder, who considered that 'the education of man on earth has been left to himself by the Godhead' who has formed humanity to fulfil his divine purpose. Carlyle was especially drawn to Schiller (who had what Coleridge called 'the material sublime' (*Table Talk*, 29 Dec. 1822)) and wrote his biography in 1824.

As the *vox Germanica* of London, Carlyle preached and practised the gospel of work. He spent fourteen years writing a history of Frederick the Great. Archetype of the upwardly-mobile autodidact, he gobbled up books in one mood and threw them up in another. He was the great anti-intellectual of his age and the effective, if involuntary opponent of French influence in England in his day. The French Revolution represented to him the end of a society and it was psychologically apt that the first volume of his study of it should have been accidentally burnt whilst in the custody of John Stuart Mill, for Mill could be regarded as a leader of the Frenchifying legion.

As mystic exponent of the superman, he insisted that 'Great men are the inspired texts of that divine Book of Revelations, whereof a chapter is completed from epoch to epoch, and by some named History' (*Sartor Resartus*, ch. 8).

Carlyle argued for universal education, 'the prime necessity of men'. Religion and education were the same to him : 'liturgies, catechisms, credos; droning thirty-nine or other articles into the infant ear' could be done by machines. It needed souls to kindle souls. Such sentiments in his essay on *Chartism* (1840) were amplified in *Past and Present* (1843). 'How dare any man', he asked his readers, referring to the Nonconformist resistance to the educational clauses of Sir James Graham's Factory Bill of that year, 'especially a man calling himself minister of God, stand up in any Parliament or place, under any pretext or delusion, and for a day or an hour forbid God's light to come into the world, and bid the Devil's Darkness continue in it one hour more!'.

Carlyle's disciples: Engels and W. E. Forster

'Under the double influence of Carlyle's *Past and Present* and of his Chartist friends' (Carr, 1934, 36), Engels wrote his famous *Condition of the Working Classes in England in 1844*. As one of Carlyle's most appreciative readers, Engels described *Past and Present* as 'the only book published in England during the past year which is worth reading'. On his way to join the German firm of Ermen and Engels in Manchester in 1842 he met Karl Marx in Paris, and on arriving in Manchester had promptly begun to write articles and reviews (from one of which the above quotation is taken). These articles for foreign newspapers were on English social and economic conditions, and so impressed Marx that he adopted from them the idea of dialectical conflict of capital and labour. They proved so satisfactory that Engels enlarged on them to write his great work.

This indictment of English industrial life, intended as a homily for Germans, became a model for English sociological research: its technique of ransacking the blue books was to be followed, not only by Marx but the Webbs as well.

Hearing that Carlyle was writing on Chartism, the Headmaster of Rugby, Dr. Arnold, wrote to tell him that he had been:

... trying, hitherto with no success, to form a Society, the object of which should be to collect information as to every point in the condition of the poor throughout the Kingdom, and to call public attention to it by every possible means. (Stanley, 1890, 371)

If Carlyle was not able to help Arnold's sociological passions, he certainly inspired Arnold's son-in-law: W. E. Forster who recommended him to his friends as 'the highest, or rather the deepest mind of the age' (*Life*, i, 155).

Five years later Forster joined with a group of Manchester business men in establishing the Lancashire Public Schools Association to promote a system of public free schools, and by 1850 they put the first of their many bills before parliament for this purpose.

Over the intervening years solid business men of Manchester with their German learners conducted a campaign in the House of Commons for a national system of education. As a result of their agitation a Royal Commission was established under the Duke of Newcastle in 1858 to 'inquire into the present state of education in England, and to consider and report what measures, if any, are required for the extension of sound and cheap elementary instruction to all classes of the people.'

The first wave of Pro-Germanists

Less articulate cases for establishing a state sytem of schools catering for children up to the age of at least fourteen were being made whilst Carlyle was thundering. In 1833 Edward Bulwer Lytton argued that universal education, under state supervision, should be made available to English children up to the age of fourteen. Bulwer Lytton (whose admiration for things German led him to send his son Edward to Bonn and not to Oxford or Cambridge), made a case in *England and the English*. He was followed by that 'true Germanized screamkin' (as Carlyle called her), Sarah Austin in 1834. Having gone to Germany with her husband, the professor of law at University College, she translated Victor Cousin's report on German schools and found the fulfilment she could never find in marriage by evangelizing for a German system of primary schools in England. Alas, this scheme was never adopted by Prussia, for Cousin obtained the scheme from Van Altenstein, the Prussian minister, but it was never enacted (Pattison, 1861, 167).

Invocation of another country is based not so much on what exists, but what people want to think exists in that country. So the features of the German scheme Sara Austin wished to emphasize were that whereas in England 'angry and ambitious' hands made religion an excuse for blocking reforms, in Prussia they were prevented by the State from doing so. She also tried to dispel 'the erroneous English notion' that the legal obligation to educate children was a modern invention of the 'military and despotic government of Prussia'. Such an obligation (*Schulpflichtigkeit*) as she showed, went back to the seventeenth century in most German states and to 1769 in Prussia. Nor did she spare the 'lifeless mechanism' of the monitorial system then used in her day by the voluntary schools. 'No German,' she wrote, 'can recommend a system of teaching, which may indeed be of use in humanizing the lowest mob of England or of France, but where men and Christians are to be formed, is defective and ill-contrived.' (Austin, 1834, xii).

She continued:

> It seems to me too, that we are guilty of great inconsistency to the ends and objects of education. How industriously have not its most able and zealous champions been continually instilling into the minds of the people, that education is the way to advancement, that 'knowledge is power', that a man cannot 'better himself' without some learning! And then we complain, or we fear, that education will set them above their station, disgust them with labour, make them ambitious, envious, dissatisfied! We must reap as we sow, (Austin, 1834, xvi–xvii)

In the same year, the Prussian model was descanted upon at large in the opening lecture to the newly formed Education Society in Glasgow, by Dr. Welsh, who praised the German concept of training teachers. German influence had been active years before—for Carlyle had been an applicant when the Scots had set up the first teachers' college in 1837. Its first principal, John M'Crie, had been sent to examine training methods in both Germany and France. It was certainly 'far in advance of anything existing in any other training institution in Great Britain' (Rich, 1933, 34).

Colleges for training both teachers and nurses together, like the institute of Protestant Deaconesses at Kaiserworth near Dusseldorf, much impressed Florence Nightingale.

Visiting it in 1850 (seventeen years after its foundation) it convinced her that nursing should be a profession, rather than a menial employment, producing ladies of the lamp rather than Sairy Gamp. She wrote an anonymous pamphlet which was printed in 1851 'by the inmates of the Ragged Colonial School at Westminster', urging the idle women of England who were 'going mad for the want of something to do' to realize the work and happiness waiting for them there. And, to test her belief, she returned there to train as one in the following year. She never lost her respect for the founder, Hans Fliedner, and was godmother to one of his children and when he died educated the child at her own expense.

Refraction from America

Sara Austin's case was reinforced by the Americans, who, as potential adopters and adapters, assessed European 'systems' in the light of their effectiveness. Two such assessments by the physicist A. D. Bache in 1839, and by the administrator Horace Mann in 1844, obtained considerable publicity in England.

Horace Mann's report was published in England in 1846 with an introduction by W. B. Hodgson who, as principal of the Liverpool Mechanics' Institute, had seen emigrants steaming away from the Mersey to the United States. Emigration was due to a lack of opportunity, and Mann indicated that the great wealth of the endowed schools and the desperate poverty of the rest was the reason why England lagged behind all the countries of Western Europe, as 'the only one, conspicuous for its civilization and resources, which has not, and never has had, any system for the education of its people.' He attributed this to the complete lack of conviction, on the part of 'men of the highest capacities and of the most extensive attainments on other subjects', that schools for the poor were needed, or, if provided, would be effective.

Thirteen years after editing Mann's *Report of an Edu-*

cational Tour in Germany (1846), Hodgson was asked to
serve on the Royal Commission on Elementary Education.
As a friend of Fichte's English biographer and translator,
William Smith, he condemned the time spent in religious
instruction. He wanted decisive state action to prevent
juvenile paupers being narcotized by neglect. Indeed the
revision of the Code of Grants in 1861 after the Newcastle Report seems to lean towards Prussian practice in
that it strongly emphasized the three R's as opposed to
other aspects of the curriculum.

The second wave of Pro-Germanists

These two American reports were read by Mark Pattison,
the Oxford don, who after a short stint as *The Times*
correspondent in Berlin in 1858, was appointed an assistant commissioner by the Newcastle Commission to report on German schools. Like Sarah Austin, Pattison
scouted the idea that compulsory schooling in Prussia was
'a creation of the modern despotic system, dictated by
philosophical sovereigns, on the ground of some abstract
theory of the right of the state over the child'. To him
Schulpflichtigkeit was not the same as *Dienstpflichtigkeit*.
Indeed it was far older, going back to the Reformation
itself (Pattison, 1861, 204-5). This overt appeal to the
Dissenters to stop suspecting compulsory education to
be an Anglican ramp was to be amplified by others, like
Matthew Arnold.

To this Commission in 1861 Pattison said that he considered that German experience had 'been longer than
ours, and has in some points passed through to stages we
are only approaching'. The history of the last 50 years
of primary instruction in Germany was to him 'a vast
storehouse of experience' which 'we cannot afford to ig-
nore' (Pattison, 1861, 168). Though 'the very foremost
feature of the educational condition of Germany at this
moment is a revival of the influence of the church and
its claims to educate the people' (1861, 171), he was

E

emphatic that the real 'cornerstone' was compulsory attendance (192). From 5 or 6 years of age, every German child spent eight or nine years at school. And though the attendance was guaranteed by law, Pattison insisted that 'this habit of universal attendance at the day school is one of the most precious traditions of German family life' and he described it as 'a religious duty before it became a law of the state'.

'Germany first, and, in the second degree, France' was Arnold's rating of the two continental models which English legislators should contemplate.

As Science, in the widest sense of the word, meaning a true knowledge of things as the basis of our operations, becomes, as it does become, more of a power in the world, the weight of nations and men who have carried the intellectual life farthest will be more and more felt. (Russell, 1901, ii, 285)

Just as Pattison reported to the Newcastle Commission on elementary education, so Arnold reported on German and French schools to the Taunton Commission on Endowed Schools. Arnold's report: *Schools and Universities on the Continent* (1868) was so successful that chapters 14–20 and 22–23, together with Appendix 10, were later published as *Higher Schools and Universities in Germany* (1882).

To Arnold Germany was an Intelligenz-Staat where 'science, not clap-trap, governs every department of human activity', and he hoped that sergeant-majors would be 'used by Geist' for higher ends. In *Friendship's Garland*, (Super 1965 v.). 'Get Geist', was the parting advice given to Englishmen by Arnold's creation Arminius, Baron von Thunder-ten-Tronckh, before setting off for the Franco-Prussian War of 1870.

Arnold's view was shared by Carlyle who rejoiced in 1870:

That noble, patient, deep, pious and solid Germany should be at length welded into a Nation, instead of vapouring, vainglorious, gesticulating, quarrelsome, restless and over sensitive France, seems to me the hopefullest public fact that has occurred in my time. (*The Times* Nov. 1870)

Wars and their lessons

'Outside events,' wrote John Morley, 'were supposed to hold a lesson. The triumphant North in America was the land of the common school. The victory of Prussians over Austrians at Sadowa in 1866 was called the victory of the elementary school teacher' (Morley, 1908, 11, 701).

The first of Prussia's three rapid conquests—that of Schleswig-Holstein—took place in 1864. The second 'that great central event, from which in every direction such momentous consequences flowed' (Morley, 1908, 746), was the defeat of the Austrians at Sadowa in 1866; the third, the even more decisive defeat of the French at Sedan in 1870.

Was England next after Denmark, Austria and France? Fears that this was so prompted the principal of the Royal Engineering College at Staines, Sir George Chesney, to write *The Battle of Dorking* (1871): an account of it happening. This moral tale on the need for 'enforced arming of the nation's manhood' swept not only Britain but Australia, Canada, New Zealand and the United States, stimulating an acrimonious debate which dragged in the Prime Minister. As a new device in the communication between a specialist group and a nation (Clarke, 1966, 47) it not only reflected the changed balance of power in Europe, but indicated a successful technique of appealing to the newly literate masses: a technique exploited with ever increasing intensity until 1914.

Certainly in the debates on clause 65 of the 1870 Education Act, the Nottingham hosiery manufacturer, A. J. Mundella, urged critics of compulsion to take a return ticket to Germany and see for themselves (*Hansard*, 8 July, 1870). But his critics derided compulsion as 'Un-

English' with the result that the school boards created by that act were only permitted—not obliged—to make bye-laws compelling children to attend school. For the next ten years, until indeed he was able, as the responsible Minister, to ensure that the school boards were obliged to compel children to attend school, Mundella kept the German example continuously before the House of Commons, so much so that he was accused of 'disparaging his own country' (*Hansard*, 21 July, 1871).

This stimulated another manufacturer, Sir Swire Smith of Keighley, to visit Germany and Switzerland in 1872, where he reported on the German scholarship ladder which led from the elementary school to the polytechnic; compulsory education till the age of 14 and the compulsory evening continuation schools for their subsequent training. But the real revelation was that Munich had more students doing research in chemistry than all the universities and colleges in Britain put together (Smith, 1873).

By 1880 Germany with a population of 42 millions was educating 6 million scholars in 60,000 schools at 2s. $11\frac{1}{2}$d. a head whilst England with a population of 34 millions was educating 3 million children in 58,000 schools at a cost of 1s. $10\frac{1}{2}$d. a head (*Annual Register*, 1880, 22).

In the same year Mundella was appointed Vice-President and secured universal compulsion by the act that bears his name. This with other innovations, like the encouragement of German teaching methods by his code of 1882 led one of his conservative predecessors to accuse him of

attempting a flight into Continental bureaucracy ... which, if Mr. Mundella's strongly avowed German preferences lead us vainly to imitate it, must fail against an antagonistic English spirit, however damaging to it the attempt may be. (Norton, 1884, 273)

Significantly enough the same journal (p. 827) which

carried this attack, also contained an account by the first Lord of the Admiralty of a new type of German cruiser (Brassey, 1884, 52).

Mundella's friend and business associate in Saxony, H. M. Felkin, went deeper than this and discovered what he considered to be the real attraction of German schools: the relevance of the curriculum and skill of the teachers. This he attributed to the ideas of the long dead Göttingen professor, Herbart. Herbart's disciples like Rein had made Jena a centre from which his ideas radiated to America and England. For Herbartianism held that nobody learnt anything by doing something else, i.e. that transfer of training (the major argument for the classics) was invalid. Children only learned as objects presented themselves to various minds at various thresholds or levels of sensation, and he suggested that the forces which attracted and repelled them could be mathematically expressed.

Herbart's wish that psychology should become a mathematical science—psycho-physics in fact, was in line with subsequent German thought. Though he became known chiefly for the logic of the way in which objects and ideas should be presented to children (the famous five steps) economic imitation spread his ideas. H.M.I.'s like F. H. Hayward, headmasters and professors like John Adams, and of course, early teacher trainers like Oscar Browning at Cambridge, M. W. Keatinge at Oxford and J. A. Finlay and C. I. Dodd at Manchester. Indeed, John Adams' *The Herbartian Psychology as applied to Education* (1897) was itself one of the earliest applications of psychology to the teaching process in the classroom.

Just how strong the movement was to imitate Germany we will now explore.

7

'Look at Germany' 1867-1914

New English Institutions

'Look at Germany' became such a ritual incantation in 1867 that Dr. Phelps, the Master of Sidney Sussex burst out 'A Prussian is a Prussian and an Englishman an Englishman, and God forbid it should be otherwise' (Winstanley, 1940, 212). He was opposing the proposal that Cambridge colleges should co-operate in the establishment of a physics laboratory. Articulating collegiate vested interests not unknown today, his words may have failed to prevent the establishment of the Cavendish laboratory, but certainly indicate why it grew so slowly. The first professor, had no place to erect his chair ... but had to 'move about like the cuckoo, depositing (his) notions in the Chemical Lecture Room in the First Term, in the Botanical in Lent, and in the Comparative Anatomy in Easter'. Even these were delivered to a very small audience. The rest of his time he spent in editing the works of the great eighteenth-century amateur scientist whose name the laboratory bore. Yet he was a distinguished physicist, none other than Clerk Maxwell.

Other universities were needed. As a parliamentary committee set up in 1867 to examine British technical instruction was told: 'a love of science and knowledge for its own sake is much more seen in those (German) universities than it is in ours' (1867–8, xv, p. 285). Not content to complain, the teller, H. E. Roscoe (then teaching chemistry at Manchester), had built up the first department of organic chemistry in the country with a German, Karl Schorlemmer as its head in 1861. Together they were to produce students like Sydney Young (who worked at University College Bristol from 1882 on hydrocarbons from petroleum), Arthur Smithells (who worked at Leeds from 1883, on improving coal gas), and German-born Arthur Schuster (who worked under Weber at Göttingen, von Helmholtz at Berlin and at the Cavendish Laboratory at Cambridge). Schorlemmer, nothing if not a fully-rounded man, was also a great friend of Engels and an internationally known socialist.

Leeds (1874) and Bristol (1876) were only two of the nine new university colleges established in the next three decades. The other six, Sheffield (1879), Birmingham (1880), Liverpool (1881), Nottingham (1881), Reading (1892), Exeter (1893) and Southampton (1902), to say nothing of three foundations in Wales, Aberystwyth (1872), Bangor (1884) and Cardiff (1883) strengthened the sinews of science teaching, especially since four of them had physicists as principals: R. T. Glazebrook (University College, Liverpool), Oliver Lodge (Birmingham), W. M. Hicks (Sheffield) and E. H. Griffiths (Cardiff).

These colleges acquired a regular apostolic succession of German trained chemists, Von Hofman's pupils taught at Mason's College, Birmingham (W. A. Tilden), Cambridge (S. Ruhemann), King's College, London (C. L. Bloxam) and Woolwich Military Academy (T. A. Abel); Bunsen's at University College, Bristol (William Ramsay), Yorkshire College, Leeds (T. E. Thorpe), Owens College, Manchester (H. E. Roscoe and Carl Schorlemmer). Pupils of other German professors like Rammelsberg (George D. Liveing), Kolbe (H. E. Armstrong) were distributed around other English colleges. A pupil of E. A. Frankland was to teach at Finsbury Technical College (R. Mendola).

The glands of economic growth

'Education among us', lamented Mark Pattison in *Suggestions on Academical Organization* (1868), 'has sunk into a trade, and, like trading sophists, we have not cared to keep on hand a larger stock than we could dispose of in the season' (Green, 1957, 248). This stock, he argued, could only be built up by establishing research as a *sine qua non* for a university appointment. 'There remains but one possible pattern on which a university, as an establishment for science, can be constructed,' he argued, 'and that is the graduated professoriate. This is sometimes called the German type.' He took the chair on 16 November, 1872, at a meeting of a short-lived Association for the Organization of Academical Study which wished to establish research as a national object (Roll-Hansen, 1957, 77–9).

With this Matthew Arnold agreed. 'Our great intellectual fault' he wrote 'is an indisposition to science—to systematic thought' (Arnold, 1874, 217). Nor was this mitigated by our school system since it seemed to breed a positive 'incapacity for science' (ibid, 207) in even the best.

Having made his name with a historical essay on the Holy Roman Empire, James Bryce now discovered that a new Holy Roman Empire was alive and the universities were its glands. 'Forty years ago', he wrote in 1885, 'an influential ecclesiastical party in England used to hold them [the German universities] up to reprobation as the parents of revolution, rationalism and pedantry. Of late years the current has run so strongly the other way that we are perhaps in danger of seeking too closely to imitate them' (Conrad, 1885, xiv). He saw students' needs in English universities: greater accessibility to middle-class students, more adequate technical instruction, recognition of the modern studies, provision for occasional students, the cultivation of research, and the better use of endowments. Here German universities offered the answers. For even though they had a higher proportion of students to population (24,187 to 45,250,000 as opposed to England's 5,500 to 26 millions) German universities also had a better staff student ratio: 1 to 11 as opposed to 1 : 30 in Scotland. English students endorsed his opinions by turning eastwards for their Ph.D.'s. Excluding those who came only for a seminar or as occasional students, there were 26 in 1835, 43 in 1860, 71 in 1880 and 159 in 1899 (Conrad, 1885, 41; U.S.A., ii, 2576).

The rich fruit of research was visible in the German *technische hochschulen*. At Karlsruhe in 1868, an internal combustion engine was built by Eugen Langen, working with Nicolaus Otto. The first professional body of German engineers, the Verein Deutscher Ingenieure, had been organized by one of its professors (F. Grashof). The existence of electromagnetic waves, and their remarkable similarity to light waves was to be proved in 1886 by another (Heinrich Hertz). Ammonia was to be synthesized by a third (F. Haber) thereby endowing Germany with enormous potential for manufacturing both fertilizers and explosives.

At a second, Stuttgart, Gottlieb Daimler was to acquire the knowledge that was to enable him to build an engine that moved at high speeds. At a third, Munich (founded in 1826), a new prime mover was born when Rudolf Deisel in 1878 decided to devote his life to the perfection of a more efficient propulsion unit that now bears his name.

At a fourth, Hanover (founded in 1831), O. Mohr had designed some of the first steel truss bridges in Germany. whilst Ludwig Prandtl was to use soap-film to solve torsion problems.

Similar case histories emerge of science being applied to the service of society. Engineering laboratories were established at *technische hochschulen* established at Dresden (1828), at Nuremberg (1829), Stuttgart (1829), Cassell (1830), Augsberg (1833) and Brunswick (1835).

When these technical universities were examined by the Royal Commission on Technical Instruction (appointed in 1881) they were found to be producing a surplus of 1,000 unemployed engineers a year, with the result that they were entering the 'learned professions' (Report, 1882, 193). With facilities for 6,000 students, these polytechnics in fact, after the establishment of the German Empire in 1871, could only register 2,000. The Commissioners were actually told by Helmholz, the great German physicist, that the number of these technical universities was 'in excess of the present requirements of the people, and had come to be so in consequence of the altered political condition of the country, which no longer consisted of separate states endeavouring to rival one another in the extent and excellence of their educational institutions' (ibid. p. 208).

An even more notable institution than all these, however, was in the process of construction, and the Commissioners reported it 'would be sufficient for the whole of North Germany'. This was the technological university at Charlottenburg, itself the result of the amalgamation of the *Bau-akadamie* (founded in 1799) and Beuth's *Gewerbeschule* (founded in 1824).

By 1899 these *technische hochschulen* were given, by imperial decree, the power to award the Dip-Ing and Dr.-Ing: equivalents of university degrees.

German practice was emulated when in 1895 Cambridge allowed graduates of other universities to register as advanced students. A system of science scholarships supervised by the Commissioners of the 1851 Exhibition was established, and from 1896 to 1921 no less than sixty of the 103 such physics scholars came to the Cavendish. In addition, a large number of workers came from the U.S.A., Germany, France, Russia and Poland. One of these 1851 exhibitioners, Ernest Rutherford, succeeded Thomson in 1919 and made the Cavendish laboratory a hatchery of physicists.

Tapping Nature's pantry

The spearhead of the German attack on Nature's pantry

was mounted in the great German chemical plants of Höchst, Ludwigshafen and Leverkusen. By 1900 they were employing 650 trained scientists to the 40 of their British counterparts (Pinson, 1966, 228). The lesson they offered, that such attacks should be mounted on a large scale, had spread to England in 1866, three years after Höchst was founded, when the German firm of Siemens transferred their small factory from Millbank to Charlton, where they built up a huge electrical engineering complex making cables (from England to India, and England to Australia), dynamos, illuminating plants and electric furnaces. Science and engineering worked so well for Siemens that in gratitude he offered to build a common hall of science for the various engineering societies, which they refused! Four years later he established a works in South Wales in 1869 to make steel by a process first devised by himself and his brother. By the time the works was abandoned in 1888 steel produced by the Siemens' process was outstripping that produced by the Bessemer process. In spite of this, British iron and steel exports began to decline from their maximum in 1882 of 4,354,000 tons to 3,263,000 tons by 1904, whilst those of Germany climbed, over the same period, from 971,000 to 2,706,000 tons (Burns, 1940, 78, 93).

Also in 1867 the German chemist Robert Ferdinand Graesser founded, with a Manchester lawyer, Timothy Crowther, a plant at Ruabon to manufacture paraffin oil and wax from colliery shale. This firm is now known as Monsanto Chemicals Ltd.

A classic example (which Bryce could not have quoted) of the influence of German chemists on British science can be seen in the English career of Carl Merkel brought over by Ludwig Mond to tutor his sons. But he soon became a figure in the firm's laboratory and in 1890 he was 'begged off' Brunner Mond's to go to Crosfields, the soap and chemical manufacturing company where he became Works Manager. He developed continental links with oil and soap firms. One consequence of this was when Crosfields began to manufacture 'Persil' by arrangement with the German firm of Henckle. He also succeeded in manufacturing pure glycerine. When Crosfields became a limited company in 1896 he was the only shareholder outside the family (Musson, 1965, 81–2).

By 1911 it was being said that men who formerly travelled in Germany selling English chemicals, now travelled in England selling German chemicals (Hoffman, 1964, 113). Certainly the German chemists were an army growing in strength year by year. A thousand of them were abroad, 400 were in the universities and another 1,500 were in other employments.

Money was being given without stint for laboratories and J. Ellis Barker, a self-appointed stimulator of the English conscience in this field, showed that German university student numbers had grown from 17,761 in 1870 to 83,089 in 1910—a rise of from 0.889 per cent per thousand inhabitants to 2.5 per cent per thousand inhabitants. In England he detected only examination-ridden ornamental and literary education. Such chemists as were produced, worked alone. As he wrote:

> Every British chemist is an island. The average work accomplished by the average British chemist is probably greater than that of his German competitor, for the Englishman puts more energy into his work, and works more quickly. Yet, though some of the greatest chemists living are Englishmen, our chemical industries are languishing owing to the lack of organized and co-ordinated effort. (Barker, 1912, 634–5)

The German clerk and the 1902 Education Act

With German pencils being used by English children, German paper being made into English government postcards, German velvets adorning English houses, German engines replacing British ones on foreign rails, and German sugar being used to sweeten English tea, a state of industrial paranoia was generated in England. So much so that English sugar barons were later to initiate the 'fair trade' movement that was to lead to protection and 'Imperial Preference'.

The mood was aptly caught by *Punch*.

> I haf brought you German culture for the poddy
> and the mind,
> *Die erhabene Kultur* of efery sort and efery kind;
> All the pessimistic dogtrines of the Schopenhauer
> school
> And the blessings of a bureaucratish-military rule.
> I shall teach you shplendit knowledge, vot you
> hitherto haf lacked,
> That religion is a fantasy, vhilst sausage is a fact;
> Ja, the mysteries of sauerkraut to you shall be
> made clear,
> And your souls shall learn to float on foaming
> waves of Lager-Bier!
>
> I do not intend to long-while you mit missionary
> rant,
> But to brighten up your intellects mit Hegel
> and mit Kant.
> Mit our Army-Service system I'll begift you
> by-and-by,
> And mit all the priceless blessings of our
> *Hohe Polizei*.
> Ach! I lofes you as a moder, and your happiness,
> I shwear,
> Shall forefer be the von surpassing object of
> my care.
> *I'll* civilise you, *Kinder*, *mid dem edlen Gerstenbrei*,
> And mit discipline, *Potztausend!*—or I'll know
> the reason vhy!
> (*Punch*, 31 January, 1885, p. 57).

In the same year, a Royal Commission was appointed to examine the causes of the depression in trade and industry in Britain. Its report indicated that tariffs and cheaper production costs were not the only reason for this depression, but that Germany, like France and Belgium had alert young business men whose technical and linguistic training was far superior to that of their English counterparts. 'Educate, educate, educate, is the burthen of the lesson from Germany—technical education for workmen and manufacturers, modern languages and science for commercial men, and manufacturers and workers alike.' So the *Spectator* on 26 June, 1886, saw the need. A couple of months later it insisted that 'There is little doubt (14 August, 1886) that the salient fact of the industrial world ... is the commercial uprising of the German people; and to this is due perhaps as much as to any more general or recorded cause the continued depression of British industry.'

Symbol of such linguistic ability, thrift and industry was the German clerk. Employed by over half the members of the Stock Exchange and thirty-five per cent of the leading city firms (*Daily Telegraph*, 25 November, 1887), he was as big a bogeyman as his brother, the German commercial traveller. 'Youths who', reported James Bryce in 1886, 'go from Germany to push their fortunes abroad are willing to live more plainly than Englishmen do, to work for smaller profits, to allow themselves fewer amusements. If they have less dash and enterprise than our countrymen, they have a steady tenacity and habits of systematic application not less valuable in the long run' (Hoffman, 1964, 87).

But as the professor of education at Manchester reminded readers of the *Fortnightly Review* in 1899 (LXVI 533) 'the German clerk, as we have learnt to know him since 1880 *has taken about sixty years to produce*; and it will take us just about as long to create a homemade article of the same quality, if we try and compete in this line.' Findlay also considered the German liking for culture and books to be very much in evidence since : 'The ordinary middle-class peasant in Germany knows more about the real nature of education and of the con-

ditions which will making schooling successful, than our
English Cabinet minister.'

Nor did the 1902 Education Act, with its accent on a
'clerkly' education, diminish this fear, for five years later
the government was giving serious consideration to a
report that 80,000 Germans, all trained soldiers, were at
work in England, a lot of them in railway stations (Young,
1963, 268).

The educationalists respond

Indeed, since 1870 educationalists had been dilating upon
the lessons Germany offered. The first professor of education to be so named and appointed in England italicized
two of them for the benefit of his English readers : *every
German elementary teacher has a separate classroom*
(Payne, 1876, p. 127) and *there are no pupil teachers in
the German primary schools* (*ibid*. p. 128). After a visit to
German schools, Joseph Payne saw nothing of the 'be-
wildered appalled look' when German schoolchildren were
asked questions and very 'little evidence' of corporal
punishment (*ibid*. pp. 132-3). Residence in Germany also
turned R. H. Quick's thoughts to teaching, and he later
went on to become one of the first teacher-trainers at
Cambridge. As he and others began to cater for intending teachers for the expanding secondary schools by
providing university courses in education, they inevitably looked to Germany, (where education (pädo-
gogik) had been a subject of study for a century),
for help. They found it in the work of Herbart
and his disciples. Their enthusiasm was fostered by
Henry Felkin, a British business man in Saxony, who
translated the master's writings, giving the emphasis to the
psychological side of his work that was to be caught up
by John Adams, another professor of education, in *The
Herbartian Psychology applied to Education* (1897).

Concerned, as such training departments were, with
assessing 'efficiency' in the classroom they adopted Her-

67

bart's techniques for correlating and concentrating lessons under five heads, basing it on his doctrine of 'apperception', and 'culture stages'. They also adopted the quantitative techniques of the German psychologist Ebbinghaus, which were, of course, refinements of those devised by the Englishman Francis Galton.

But it was Herbart who held the stage, together with his followers Stoy and Rein. Stoy's 'seminar' in pedagogy at Jena, founded in 1842, was so developed after his death in 1885 by Dr. Rein, his successor, that it enrolled one-tenth of the total number of students in the university. It was based on three principles: *Theoretikum*, *Pratikum* and the Conference. The first dealt with problems, the second was a demonstration lesson given (and criticized by the students), whilst the third, presented by Rein himself, involved the discussion of the criticisms. Rein's own convictions were described as 'chiefly modern Christian socialism' (Dodd, 1898, 192).

English educationalists in the main followed Rein's methodology of the lesson, which became famous as the five Herbartian 'Steps', familiar in all lesson notes of students.

1. Preparation (*Vorbereitung*)
2. Presentation (*Darbietung*)
3. Association (*Verknüpfung*)
4. Formulation or Generalization (*Zusammenfassung*)
5. Application (*Anwendung*)

To Miss C. I. Dodd, a tutor in an English Training Department, Herbartanism was 'an expansion of the great law of proceeding from particular to the general and back again to the particular' (Dodd, 1898, 9, 123–135), whilst to F. H. Hayward it 'alone could inspire, move and fascinate' those who wished to galvanize the 'paralytic condition of education in England' (Hayward, 1903 p.v.).

German social legislation

'We stand today' opined *The Times* in a leading article

on 4 October, 1906 'in the position of an industrially underdeveloped country trading with another country on a far higher level of industrial efficiency.' The German Navy Bill of the same year in which six battleships and the widening of the Suez Canal were planned, alarmed the British who could not see it as anything other than a threat. So Haldane, as Minister of War, organized the British army as an expeditionary force, and established a general staff, whilst Fisher did the same for the navy.

Unwilling to squander money 'on building gigantic flotillas to encounter mythical armadas', and preferring to ensure more basic national efficiency, Lloyd George— who became Chancellor of the Exchequer in 1908— visited Germany to examine its system of contributary national insurance against its health and old age. This he adopted in his budget by forcing through the principle of the taxation on land values and in the course of it, severely curtailing the powers of the House of Lords (Jones, 1951, 36).

Indeed the Fabian doctrine of the national minimum in efficiency through health and education was modestly but effectively implemented by his colleagues: the Education (Provision of Meals) Act of 1906, The Medical Inspection of Children Act of 1907; the Employment of School Children Outside School Hours Act 1908; and the Housing and Town Planning Act of 1909.

In these, as in the provision of school medical attention and in the raising of the school leaving age, the pacemaker was Germany, but the speed and direction of the course she was setting led to a head-on collision in 1914.

An English doctor regarded such progress as kangaroo-like and complained that in matters like national insurance, as in motors and aeroplanes:

we wait to use the experience of others; we then give a mighty leap and land ahead of those who have inspired our move; and there we stick until the world has again gone past us. In wise and liberal expenditure on education and research, and again in imperial organisation, we are

F

far behind the German Empire and the United States. (Fremantle, 1914, 369)

Haldane: the Germanophile

To avert the head-on collision the most pro-German minister of the century was sent to Berlin in 1912. He went there under the pretence of examining technical education.

There was a double irony in this, since Richard Burdon Haldane had previously organized the territorial army, and was also known for his belief that technical and philosophic training could and should not be pursued in separate institutions. This theme he had been pursuing for fourteen years, ever since he had, with Sidney Webb, secured the establishment of the Imperial College of Science and Technology on the model of Charlottenburg, as well as refashioning, against the wishes of many of the professors of London, a teaching university. Elsewhere in England universities were small, 'Lilliputian' was the phrase attributed to Bryce. Neither Bryce nor Matthew Arnold would have had them otherwise lest they prejudice the 'idea of a university'. Haldane was 'of a different opinion' (Haldane, 1929, 140) and persuaded himself 'that a Civic University was a possible institution, and that if called into being it would have a great moulding influence.' His views were shared by Joseph Chamberlain, another pro-German, who incidentally had earlier worked for an alliance between Germany, Britain and the United States—a sort of Atlantic compact.

At Haldane's suggestion a strong Privy Council committee was set up which granted charters to Liverpool and Manchester and encouraged Leeds to petition for one. Charters for other universities followed: Sheffield in 1905 and Bristol in 1909. Aptly enough when Haldane was elected Chancellor of Bristol in 1912 he delivered an address on 'The Civic University'.

German generosity to English colleges

It is hard indeed at this point of time, to gainsay the influence of Germans on English academic life before the First World War. To the universities, the great German firm of Wernher Beit and Co. gave very large sums of money to establish German type scientific training in England: Imperial College being only one of the recipients. In the provinces, German merchants were very active in schools. Thus at Nottingham, a member of the German colony tried to remodel Nottingham High School. Securing the convention of a special mayoral meeting in 1888, Bernhard Stiebel criticized the autocracy of the headmaster and the school's devotion to Latin. But his ideas, which included the training of teachers, the appointment of assistants by the governors and the employment of good speakers of foreign languages found no favour (Thomas, 1957, 222).

Similar case-histories could be advanced all over the country. Well might Michael Sadler, who as a Civil Servant provided comparative studies with a centre when he set up the Department of Special Inquiries and Reports in 1892, and who as Professor of Education at Manchester did so much for the continuation school movement, write in 1912:

> what the English government is now doing for the organization of secondary schools and for the subsidizing of university studies is in great measure traceable to German example and to the effects of German experience upon English opinion.

For to nineteenth- and early twentieth-century English liberals, the Germans were accorded 'special honours in comparison with other foreigners' as 'clean, industrious, and ardent social democrats' (Muggeridge, 1964, 21). But to right-wingers and conservatives, however, Germany was a menace to Church, State, England, and indeed, civilization. They listened, approved, and acted on the promptings of the greatest Germanophobe of them all:

Lord Northcliffe, whose *Daily Mail* contributed by its quota of alarmist reports to the first disastrous escalation of modern times: the 1914–1918 war, which, as Lloyd George said, no one at the head of affairs quite wanted.

8

The lessons of World War I

State initiative expands

When the British army went to war with them in 1914 the full magnitude of the German achievement was felt. For the khaki dye of the British soldiers' uniforms, the glass of their rangefinders, the fuses of their shells, the magnetos for their trucks, the drugs in their hospitals, and the aspirins of their generals were all German, or manufactured under German licence. So the Board of Trade appointed German-trained Lord Haldane to chair a committee to 'advise as to the best means of obtaining for the use of British industries, sufficient supplies of chemical products, colours and dyestuffs of kinds largely imported from countries with which we are at present at war.'

On result of this was that to obtain the coal tar derivatives like benzene, naphthalene and anthracene, which had been so fully exploited in Germany that they virtually controlled the world production, the Government gave £1,500,000 to help form a new company, British Dyes Ltd. (later the British Dyestuffs Corporation).

Science in government

Within four months of the outbreak of war the universities branch of the Board of Education had prepared a memorandum making proposals for increasing the facilities to train scientists and research workers. This was considered by the Presidents of the Board of Trade and of Education who were urged by the Royal Society and other scientific societies to establish a National Chemical Advisory Committee to foster closer relations between industry and the universities and between applied and pure scientists. From these ideas grew the Advisory Council for Scientific Research and Development: the first indication that the Government was now definitely committed to foster industrial research. Its instrument, fashioned in 1916, was the Department of Scientific and Industrial Research (now known as the Science Research Council).

Among the several features of this plan, which were 'without precedent in British practice,' one was that 'technical advice to the responsible Minister was placed permanently in commission and entrusted to a permanent body of independent and distinguished men of science and other industrialists, and not to officials either of the Committee itself or of other Departments of State' (Heath and Hetherington, 1946, 252).

Science in schools

To recruit researchers more science was needed in schools. So a powerful committee was appointed in 1916 by the prime minister under Sir J. J. Thomson to advise on the measures needed to promote the study of science in secondary schools and universities. It found 'no need now to labour the important part this science should play in our education', but it noted 'memories are short and it may be well to register in formal words for future comfort, if not reproach, what all would readily grant at this moment.'

That registration, in some 83 recommendations, brought the schools yet further into line with German practice: the compulsory state inspection of all schools, a 'revolution in the public attitude' to the training of teachers, the adoption of the metric system, and the raising of the school leaving age to 16.

Perhaps the most astringent comment of the Thomson Committee was on the heuristic method. Practitioners of this method insisted, like its great advocate the German-trained chemist, H. E. Armstrong, that pupils should 'discover by their own experiments, with little or no suggestion from the teacher, the solutions of problems set to them or of problems which they themselves suggest': a supposition the Committee described as wasting the time and opportunities of pupils (p. 56).

Indicating (p. 114) the startling discrepancy in the number of full-time students of engineering and technology in English universities and technical colleges (2,686) as opposed to their counterparts in German Technische Hochschulen and Bergakademien (11,690), the Thomson Committee insisted that 'the crux of the situation was the nature and prevalence of education of secondary grade' for they wished for 'all pupils to gain some further knowledge of Science both in its more general aspects and in its bearing on industry' (p. 119–120).

In a prescient aside they saw no reasons why 'three fingers were put into the secondary pie' (p. 127) and suggested that the 'water-tight divisions' between the inspectorate of the Junior Technical Schools, the Central Schools and the Secondary Schools should be abolished.

They also wished for improved accommodation and equipment in Technical Schools—some of which they considered should be 'Local Colleges'. This meant that 'in the not too distant future new institutes' would 'have to be built and many of the existing buildings enlarged and improved' (p. 120).

The need for technical education to be liberalized by the inclusion of courses in pure science and of studies like economics and sociology, enabling a student to orient himself in the community, was stressed by yet another committee, this time of the Ministry of Reconstruction (Cmd. 321, 1919, pp. 174–5). So impressed had they been by the success of adult education in the army following experiements at Brocton and Rugeley that they recommended its continuance and extension to peacetime life. They also proposed to enhance the rôles of universities local authorities and the voluntary provision of other forms of adult education. Universities were to be given funds to establish departments of extra-mural education; local authorities to be obliged to submit to the central government an indication of their plans, and the voluntary societies helped by both. Moreover they suggested that at a cost of £5 million the state should recreate the rural communities through a system of village institutes under full public control (*ibid*. p. 170–173).

'There is some danger' wrote its chairman to the prime minister, 'of all organization, especially educational organization being regarded as Prussianism ... some of the best lessons are those taught by the enemy and the lesson we have to learn is how to combine ... freedom and individuality with a good deal more efficiency and system and organization.... Never was the lesson more needed than now' (Cmd. 321, 1919, v).

The rise of modern studies

Sir J. J. Thomson's Committee stressed that even in small towns where there was room for only one secondary school, 'opportunities for learning one foreign language should be provided'. This argument was taken up with even greater verve by another committee appointed at the same time to enquire into the Position of Modern Languages in the Educational System of Great Britain. This reported that

The war has made this people conscious of its ignorance of foreign countries and their peoples.... The masses and the classes alike were ignorant to the point of public danger ... of the mental attitude and aspirations of the German people.

Such ignorance, it considered, 'prevented due preparation and hampered our efforts after the war had begun; it still darkens our counsels'. So the committee suggested that teaching of the languages, together with history, literature and economic development of Germany, France, Italy and Russia, should be improved.

'During the early part of this century the study of German was not going forward but backward' it reported, and continued 'It is of essential importance to the nation that the study of the German language should be not only maintained, but extended (p. 62). So should Spanish, Russian and Italian'. The committee, which had as its secretary A. E. Twentyman, one of Sadler's young men, found it 'not easy to believe that the 205 Classical Scholars and Exhibitioners elected in 1911–12 by the Colleges of Oxford and Cambridge were all worth their salt', especially since out of a total of 440 scholarships only 8 were awarded in modern languages (p. 153). They concluded that 'no part of our national education has remained so far below the standard of national and individual requirement as that which is concerned with foreign countries and foreign peoples of the present day, and which employs living languages as its instrument' (p. 209) and urged that they be developed as an integral part of a modern studies course, with 'rewards and facilities' equal to those afforded to Greek and Latin, the compulsory teaching of which they considered were 'a special impediment to the study of modern languages and to the further studies based upon these' (p. 212).

But the recommendation that compulsory Greek and Latin should be abolished for Arts degrees was but one of the fifty-three: others included subventions for students to spend some time abroad, that oral tests on, and the direct method of teaching, modern languages should be developed and that a translation test should be available to mathematicians and scientists, and that support for some 55 chairs and 110 lectureships should be found by the government (p. 221). Above all they recommended the establishment of 'a strong and competent Advisory Committee' to help in this.

One of its most interesting recommendations was that a committee should be set up to consider the potentialities of artificial languages. For the two which then held the stage were *Esperanto*, devised by Dr. L. L. Zamenhof in 1887 and its offspring IDO, devised in 1907. One had a limited vocabulary, whilst the other 'imperilled such common accord as Esperanto had achieved' (*ibid*, 70).

This problem engaged the English psychologist, C. K. Ogden. From a preoccupation with the meaning of meaning, he went on to devise a technique for basic English through a select vocabulary of 850 words.

Continuation schools

In 1914 Ogden had translated the work of Georg Kerschensteiner, who, as director of education for Munich, had established a superb network of continuation schools.

The imposition of compulsory part-time attendance at such schools in England and Wales for 320 hours up to the age of 18 was recommended by a Departmental Committee under J. Herbert Lewis.

In that same year H. A. L. Fisher, who knew Germany well, became the President of the Board of Education. Just as he had courageously refused to bow to the hysterical patriots, and forbid the teaching of German in schools, so he now strongly supported the idea of compulsory (as opposed to evening) continuation schools for children from 15 to 18, as popularized by Dr. Georg Kerschensteiner, and for whose establishment educationists like Michael Sadler, economists like H. A. Clay and industrialists like R. H. Best of Birmingham and T. C. Horsfall of Manchester had argued. For in Germany, attendance at continuation classes was compulsory for children from 14 to 17 years of age, and, where no schools were available, travelling teachers went from village to district.

Though Fisher's aided continuation schools were axed by the Geddes Committee, and though Sections 42 and 43 of the 1944 Act also fell by the wayside, they have been revived and reclothed by the Crowther Report and the reorganizations following circular 10/65. Indeed, present colleges of further education owe much to such stimuli.

Making room for merit

Perhaps one of the reasons why the continuation school failed to engage national attention in England was that the national need demanded that resources be concentrated to discovering pupils of ability.

'The belief has been spread in neutral countries' reported the Consultative Committee of the Board of Education in 1916 'that we have entered upon this war with the hope that we might crush German trade and industry by force, since we could not by peaceful means withstand its growing pressure' (Cmd. 8291, 1916, p. 4). Whilst discounting this, a group of its members did stress that the war had 'forced the breach in tradition which gives a chance to a new spirit and new methods' (*ibid*, p. 5).

In this 'new spirit' though the committee questioned whether the existing scholarship system was 'either necessary or useful' (p. 66) they concluded it was essential since public education was not 'compulsory, gratuitory and uniform' (p. 9). They recommended the universal extension of scholarships from elementary schools to junior technical schools and on throughout the system, as well as the prolongation of scholarships at the university.

Since the annual state provision for universities in Germany was, in the immediate pre-war years, six times greater than that afforded in England and Wales:

£1,500,000 as opposed to £265,000, the committee recommended that the Central Government, not the Local Authorities should shoulder the additional expense of providing for the greatly extended system of mainten-ance grants, proposed for students to strengthen the upper forms of schools, and scholarships to cover not only undergraduate but postgraduate courses.

And perhaps too the accent on the identification and cosseting of youth of high academic ability was to lead to others reacting in anti-intellectual ways which we shall now explore.

9

Youth Movements, 1919-1955

The Youth Hostel movement

A sentiment, long manifest among many Englishmen who
would have been horrified at Hitler's racist ideas, was
that of robust anti-intellectualism and rejection of the
over complicated machine age. Young ramblers, encouraged to roam the fells before the First World War
by radical newspapers like the *Clarion*, turned to roam
Germany. Individualistic and anti-militarist, they scorned
drugs and alcohol, and warmed to the similar groups they
found on the Continent, especially the *Verband für
Deutsche Jugend herbergen*, a body formed by a Westphalian teacher, Herr Richard Schirrman, who from 1907
had been providing paliasses in classrooms for young
ramblers. By 1913 he had succeeded in establishing a
number of one night shelters—*jugendherbergen*.

After the First World War these shelters began to be
much used by English ramblers abroad, especially those
from the large conurbations like Bristol and Merseyside
and it was a party of ramblers returning to the latter area
that voiced the need for similar shelters in England
(Moorhouse, 1936, xvii). Their rôle in preserving the
countryside attracted the Council for the Preservation
of Rural England, just as their accent on health attracted
the newly formed British Youth Council. Some forty soci-

eties like Toc H (a wartime fellowship), the Y.M.C.A., and the Workers' Travel Association saw the need, and attended a conference organized in 1930 by the National Council of Social Service, at which the National Association to promote Youth Hostels was launched, the name Youth Hostels being a direct translation of *jugendherbergen*.

Anglo-German youth

> They seemed to me to have a certain delicacy of touch in life which was in themselves and not dependent on their surroundings, and which should, if it can be transplanted, go far to solve the problem of which the Labour Movement (among others) has to face of providing a life which is not based on luxury, and which yet escapes beastliness and dullness.

So David Ayerst summed up his impressions of the German students' expedition to Northumbria in September 1927, confessing that he 'personally had learnt very much from them' (Gardiner and Rocholl, 1928, 275). 'Their greatest lesson for us,' he continued, 'was the feeling of repose and of the dignity of Nature.'

That visit was the climax of several successful earlier ones. Youth groups like the *Märkische Spielgëmeinde* had toured Southern England in 1926; the *Jungmannschaft* of the German *Bünde* had toured Northumbria in 1927; and the German Singers, helped by the National Union of Students, had toured most major towns in England in 1928.

Led by a thirty-one year old former elementary school teacher Georg Goetsch, these groups, like the *Alt-Wandervögel*, to which he belonged, owed much to the *Deutsche Freischar*. These bodies, the *Bund der Wandervögel und Pfadfinder*; the *Deutsche Pfadfinder Bund*; the *Jungnationaler Bund*; and the *Märkische Spielgëmeinde* supported the publication of a record of Anglo-German discussions: *Ein Neuer Weg* (1927) to synchronize with the arrival of fifty members of the German Youth Movement for a camp on the Scottish border and subsequently for a series of festivals in Northumbria. The National Union of Students simultaneously commended the English translation to its readers.

Members of the Symposium included a master at Repton (Alec MacDonald), a journalist on the *Manchester Guardian* (Kingsley Martin), the Professor of Music at Cambridge (E. J. Dent) and other notables like Dr. G. P. Gooch. These were matched on the German side by the founder and director of the student exchange organization (*Deutscher-Akademischer Austauschdienst*, formed in 1925), the Professor of Geography at Hanover (Professor Erich Obst), the Professor of Law at Breslau (Eugen Rosenstock) and other former army officers, civil servants and journalists.

It was in this that David Ayerst's remarks were printed.

These interchanges seem, in retrospect, to have had the reverse effect to what was intended, in that German students became even more aware of their own handicaps.

> The really dangerous political fact we were always coming up against in our discussions, [said John Laiyard] was the feeling that the Germans now have, more than ever before the War, of being hemmed in, with no room for political or individual expansion . . . an English student with energy and capability, if unable to find employment in England, could invariably get a job in one of the Dominions or Colonies, whereas for a German there was no such outlet unless he lost his nationality. (ibid., 279)

Furthermore, as Gerhard Müller (the director of the *Holstenschule* in Neumünster Schleswig-Holstein) sadly confessed to the existence in Germany of an intellectual proletariat caused partly by this very reason (ibid., 207–8). For it intensified and aggravated the worship of certificates, a fetish known as *berichtigungswesen*, and drove German parents to exhort their children to get *Reifezeugnis* at any price.

Müller argued that a future 'Dictator of Education' was needed to cut back such excesses, and introduce a common course up to ten, followed by four successive choices at ten, twelve, fourteen and sixteen. 'Even if we never come to the point of having a formal Dictator' he argued, 'the German school system must inevitably develop, in the direction of simplification and increased utility' (ibid., 209–10).

The chief promoter of these discussions and tours was Rolf Gardiner. Towards the end of the War he had, at Bedales, burst into print with some poems subsequently published in Vienna as *The Second Coming* (1922). After organizing these tours he set up the Anglo-German Academic Bureau at 58 Gordon Square, London W.C. 1, where he issued *In Northern Europe*, the first (and only) volume of which appeared in 1930. This Bureau had no connection with the Anglo-German Club, or the even more notorious Anglo-German Information Service subsequently established to distribute Nazi propaganda.

Gardiner went on to argue that it was not the 'pot-pourri of Mussolini, Hitler, Lenin and the public school spirit that would cure the malady of the British spirit but an emulation of the German Bund—an élite like the men in John Buchan's story *Midwinter* who would exert power in the lanes and hamlets of England' and whose authority would be 'as anonymous as the seasons' (1932, 38).

D. H. Lawrence

In a letter to Gardiner on 7 January, 1928, D. H. Lawrence lamented:

It is very difficult to do anything with the English: they have so little 'togetherness', or power of togetherness: like grains of sand they will only fuse if lightning hits it. The Germans take their shirts off and work in the hay: they are still physical: the English are so woefully disembodied. God knows what's to do with them. I sometimes think they are too sophisticatedly civilized to have any future at all. (Gardiner, 1932, 35)

To Gardiner, Lawrence's works were the 'pebbles of prophecy' especially *The Plumed Serpent, Ramon* and *Cipriano.* Lawrence himself, visiting Germany four years earlier had detected a 'a queer *bristling* feeling of uncanny danger coming out of the air'. He detected the abreaction of youth against the shabby asphalt of mechanization and urged a return to the breast and the womb. He suggested that the common man could:

> give me back the responsibility for general affairs, a responsibility which he can't acquit, and which saps his life. I would like him to give me back the responsibility for thought, for direction.... I would undertake my share of the responsibility if he gave me his belief.

In *Fantasia of the Unconscious* (p. 72) he gave a blueprint for an age to be:

> All schools will shortly be converted either into public workshops or into gymnasia.... Active training in primitive modes of fighting and gymnastics will be compulsory for all boys over ten years of age.... The great mass of humanity should never learn to read and to write—never. First and foremost establish a rule over them, a proud, harsh manly rule.

Lawrence, a rootless intellectual like so many Germans, was caught up in the Lagardeian-Nietzschean simplification of life that found favour in the Germany of the 'twenties. His relationship with Germany was as 'both more intimate and more critical than that of any other English writer' (Gray, 1965, 340). Before the first war whilst seeing his professor at Nottingham to solicit his help in obtaining an assistantship at a German university, he had absconded with his professor's wife, also a German. Like Germany, Lawrence had been treated as an outlaw ever since. And it is impossible to treat persons like outlaws or aborigines without awakening them to the advantages of behaving in that way. As with Lawrence, so with Germany one catches an 'artificial simplification of economic and political concepts, the resurrection of the warrior and of the creed of physical force as the ultimate ratio' (Kotschnig, 1937, 285).

The Hungerkandidaten

There were many Lawrences in Germany: 'What a dangerous mass of inflammatory, revolutionary material and social embitterment are heaping themselves up now in those old homes of German culture' exclaimed Dibelius (Kotschnig and Prys, 1932, 68). To him the German universities had become 'a temporary haven of those who would otherwise sink to the proletariat'. Their number was a symbol of 'dire distress', whilst Sir Ernest Barker complained that 'too large a population' congested the universities, lowering the standard of instruction. 'It may tend,' he went on, 'to produce an unemployed, or uncongenially and inadequately employed, intellectual proletariat; and an intellectual proletariat is the seed-bed of revolutionary movements, political and economic' (Kotschnig and Prys, 1932, 104).

So Germany became for England an object lesson in what Sir Ernest Barker called 'the revolutionary force' of 'the discontented product of a clerkly system of education' (Barker, 1922, 244). Whereas English university enrolments had risen from 27,728 in 1913 to 47,826 in 1930, in Germany they had risen over the same period from 76,847 to 132,690. More graphically the number of British university students only rose by 6,220 in the five years before 1930 (i.e. nearly 15 per cent), whereas in Germany over the same period they rose by 42,609 (i.e. an increase of 50 per cent) (Kotschnig, 1937, 13). For by 1932 Germany had 1 student to every 690 of the population to Britain's 1 to 1,150. These German students could not get posts commensurate with their training; by the late

1920's 25,000 were leaving universities each year com-
peting for half that number of positions. This shortage of
posts bred resentment amongst the jobless and swelled the
numbers of the academic proletariat who looked with
jaundiced eyes on democracy (Struve, 1965, 1044).

Moreover they were adrift in a far more status-
conscious world. In Germany the proportion of salaried
employees to wage-workers had decreased from 1:21
(in 1882) to 1:9 (in 1907) to 1:4 (in 1925). These new
middle-class workers were 'little men' as Hans Fallada saw
them, in his novel (*Kleiner Mann. Was nun?* Berlin,
1932). For those who had jobs were terrified of losing this
status. Their parents, as the first victims of post-war in-
flation, also suspected the apparent co-operation of 'big'
business and 'big' labour that made up the Weimar Republic.

Their ears were all attuned to hear who was responsible for their troubles and they soon heard: the Jews.

Hitlerism

Blamed in Russia before, and blamed for the Communist
revolution of 1917, the Jews were widely believed to be
working through 'democracy', 'liberalism' and socialism
to establish world Zionism (or Communism) under their
Elders, whose *Protocols* (a pre-war Russian forgery) had
been brought to Germany by Russian émigrés and exploited for publicity purposes by one of Hitler's mentors:
Alfred Rosenberg. Soviet-judaea became the target for the
Nazi party. There *lebensraum* would be found. And, to
convince England and France that Germany was the last
bulwark against the 'Red Flood', he stressed that, unless
checked, 'Bolshevism would change the world as com-
pletely as Christianity did'.

Hitler was a symbol of progress through collective
belief rather than through individual painstaking effort:
'In him,' wrote Malcolm Muggeridge, 'each unrealized
self could find realization, none frustrated, self-expression

available for all, instead of only in co-educational schools, University Extension classes, and other places which specialized in facilitating it' (Muggeridge, 1967, 266).

Hitler solved the unemployed student problem. By 1937 numbers had shrunk just over half the 1932 total. Those in mathematics and natural sciences had shrunk to 35.6 per cent of the 1932 figures, modern languages to 23.4 per cent and classics to 35.6 per cent. But students of education rose to 142.5 and of journalism 169.7 per cent of the 1932 numbers in those fields. (*Nature*, CXLII, 175, 1938). All this was accompanied by a nationalistic cult of masculinity and Aryanism described by W. H. Auden as 'the hitherto-unconscious creed of little men who half succeed'.

As early as 1924 the readers of the prestigious *Hibbert Journal* were told that:

> Hitler represents healthy reaction against capitalism on the basis of the new mediaevalism. His social theory has much in common with the Guild movement in England, and the success that has followed his activities is a sign of the times. (Hübener, 1924, 71)

This view was shared by many Englishmen. The fitness rallies and the public service stints seemed evidence that not all Germans were Spenglerians, and were doing their utmost to arrest the decay of the Aryans and the decline of the West. Indeed the editor of the *Hibbert Journal* became the president of the Secondary Schoolmasters' Physical Training Association which stemmed from a course run by two H.M.I.'s (both former Army officers) in 1924.

There was a considerable amount of sympathy with what Hitler was professing to do. Subconscious memories stirred of Joseph Chamberlain's pre-war dream of an Anglo-German-American alliance, and of his friend Professor Ashley's opinion that 'Germany and England are naturally marked out to be friends by their position in face of the United States and Russia' (Ashley, 1903, p.

197). Others put it down to 'Cecil Rhodes' insistent and ignorant pan-Germanism' manifest in the 'All Souls' group controlling *The Times* (Rowse, 1961, 115).

As the Nazis' capture and channelling of the enthusiasm of youth became apparent, it seemed as if a Boy Scout Germany was in process of being moulded. For the Hitler youth were organized from 10 to 14 as *Jungvolk* or *Jungmadel* and from 14 to 18 as the *Hitler jugend* or the *Bund Deutscher Mädchen*. Those exhibiting special prowess as 'leaders' would be able to climb a ladder from the Adolf Hitler School, to the Napola (*National Politische Erziehungsanstalt*) then to the *Ordenstburgen*, and finally to a projected National Socialist University on Lake Chiernsie in Bavaria: a kind of superior Baden Powell type Chilwell.

Many Englishmen approved of this. Student labour, the sense of high destiny, and selection of an élite through a strenuous rather than an intellectual life seemed to be an extension of practices then unhappily being abandoned in England. Thus to Sir Arnold Wilson, Hitler's youth policy was 'actuated by the same motives as those which inspired Dr. Arnold, but applied to a whole nation, not to a class, with the same emphasis on character, physique and general culture rather than on pure intellect and special knowledge' (Marlowe, 1967, 353).

As editor of the prestigious journal *The Nineteenth Century and After*, and as an M.P., Sir Arnold Wilson spoke for many Englishmen when he attacked intellectuals, the League of Nations and Socialists, and approved of youth hostels, agricultural labourers and the lower middle classes. Particularly did he like the idea of all professors and university students doing a ten weeks stint in a work camp: an egalitarian operation that won his entire approval. The Nazis, by their refusal to consider class distinction in the drive for fitness and instillation of a sense of purpose in the nation, seemed to be doing the right thing.

With England meeting the same problem of the unemployed as Germany (it hovered between one and two millions from 1921 to 1939), national action to prevent physical deterioration was necessary. Every German city had, between 1923 and 1930, built vast sports stadia, but the English preferred to organize voluntary groups like the National Playing Fields Association (in 1925), or the Women's League of Health and Beauty (in 1935). However, voluntary effort could not match what had become by 1937 a formidable challenge, so with a flurry of White Papers the Government in that year set up a National Advisory Council for Physical Training and Recreation with twenty-two subsidiary area committees. Shrewd observers approved of it as a necessary concomitant of the armaments programme. In the same year a Physical Training and Recreation Act was passed whereby a National Fitness Council, with £2 million to be spent over three years, was set up.

Kurt Hahn

Three years later came exiles driven from Germany by Hitler's intolerance. One of them was Kurt Hahn, formerly headmaster of Salem, who arrived in England in the summer of 1933. Later in the year Gordonstoun was founded around him. This became much more a diffuser of 'health-giving habits of life' than Hahn's own German School, Salem. Within three years it had, with Elgin Academy, joined forces to institute a series of tests in athletics, expeditions, life-saving and self-discipline. Successful candidates obtained a Moray Badge. This led to the National Fitness Council running summer schools and short residential courses. When war broke out in 1939 the Moray Badge system received endorsements in *The Times*. A County Badge Experimental Committee was set up. From this stemmed the idea of 'Outward Bound' schools offering short-term toughening courses for all boys. The first of these was organized at Aberdovey in 1941 with Jim Hogan helped by Dr. Zimmermann, formerly director of Physical Education at Göttingen. This was followed by another at Burghead, begun in 1948. Two mountain schools were also established at Eskdale (1950) and Ullswater (1955). One of Hahn's pupils, Prince Philip, later Duke of Edinburgh, extended the idea with his awards scheme.

The arms of America

'The sudden appearance of Germany as the grizzly terror' had, in the opinion of an American, effected what the Adamses had tried for two hundred years to do—frightened England into America's arms (Adams, 1928, 363). The 'grizzly terror' made itself manifest, not only in the massed rallies, the goose-stepping and the persecutions as in the overt organizations—fifth columns—designed to influence the English, like for instance, the *Deutscher Europäischer Kulturbund*. Other organizations were set up in Germany for less sophisticated persons.

Between the Zoo and the American Embassy in Berlin there was established in October 1935 an Anglo-German Fellowship, and a *Deutsch-Englische Gesellschaft* to promote better understanding. This followed the promotion of inter-academic visits and the establishment of the German Institute: both results of the *Deutscher Akademischer Austauschdienst*.

A subtler corrupter was the Link, founded in July 1937. Of the 35 branches in 1939, the largest was in Birmingham, with 4,000 members linked by the *Anglo-German Review*.

For this reason a number of English writers, who also rejected materialism, chose to go to America: W. H. Auden and Christopher Isherwood especially. Both of these hailed Kafka as showing the Communist generation of interwar Britain the way back to individualism and a world of transcendental values. In their *The Ascent of F6* (1936) W. H. Auden hailed him as the 'Columbus' of the individual in an age of machines. 'It is fit and proper' he wrote (*The Wandering Jew*, 1941, ii, 186), 'that Kafka should have been a Jew, for the Jews have for a long time been placed in the position in which we are now all to be: of having no home.' To Edwin Muir, translating Kafka's *Castle*, it was 'a sort of modern Pilgrim's progress'. Certainly Kafka's influence on Graham Greene, William Sansom and Rex Warner has been profound, and these, in an age of mass literacy, are an education in themselves.

10

The two economic miracles 1945-1968

The first: West Germany

In spite of being divided into eleven *Länder* (reduced to
nine in 1952 and raised to ten in 1957), a network of
national consultative and co-operative bodies has been
established in the West German Federal Republic. A
Permanent Conference of the Ministers of Culture of the
Länder (set up in 1948) has various executive committees
for schools, universities, and art training. Another keeps
the Ministers appraised of developments abroad. A Conference of University Rectors (like the British Committee
of Vice-Chancellors) was first convened in the British, then
in the American, and then in the French zone. A German
Education Committee, sponsored jointly by the Federal
Government and the *Länder* was set up in 1953, and, four
years later, a Science Council. The recommendations of
the latter seemed by 1963 to have acquired the authority
of fiats (Hiscocks, 1966, 165). Flanked by a Ministry for
Scientific Research (created in 1962 from the Ministry for
Nuclear Power), the organization is tight and homogenous
considering the difficulties of the *Länder*.

As ingenious exponents of the art of securing the
maximum use of minimal educational equipment the
Germans have set a fast pace in Europe. Though well
down the O.E.C.D. League table of nations in the amount

of the gross national product spent on education in 1958–9 (2.79 per cent as compared to the 3.67 per cent of the United Kingdom or 4.53 of the U.S.A.), they are probably at its head where plant utilization is assessed. Up till 1956 they operated a shift-system in the schools—a relic of post-war improvization—and up until 1962 an exceptionally low ratio of staff to students in the universities.

Here the 'overview' of the Permanent Conference's Report of 1962 (a year before the Robbins Report in England) gave a realistic assessment of needs by 1970 when it expected educational expenditure to be more than doubled (from 9 milliard to 19.9 milliard marks).

With imports nearly quintupled and exports more than sextupled over the years 1950 to 1963 the Federal Republic of Germany stood, compared with the United Kingdom, on equal terms with regard to the first and ahead on the second. Moreover, its overseas aid was almost as much as Britain's—226 millions as opposed to 241 millions.

Certainly West Germany's rate of growth was startlingly larger than that of the U.K.: 6.5 per cent per annum as opposed to 2.2 per cent. If such a rate of growth were to continue, it was calculated that the average Gross National Product of Germany would overtake that of the U.S.A. in 1979, whereas that of the United Kingdom would not do so until 2086 (Boulding, 1967, 58).

All this has a sound manpower base, rising from an organized educational system.

Its educational base

Though German universities, unlike their British counterparts, rode on a pre-war rise and a post-war fall in the birthrate, yet they more than doubled their student enrolment between 1950 (110,820) and 1962/3 (234,680). Also unlike Britain, the fifteen pre-war German universities had been academically weakened before, as well as physically damaged during, the war. (Kiel, for instance, had to restart in some ships in the harbour). Nor did bitter memories of graduate unemployment inhibit the foundation of new ones, six of which (Berlin, Mainz, Saarbrücken, Bochum, Regensburg and Bremen) took shape in the first two post-war decades. Comparing them with British universities, one German noted that they had

> an advantage which isn't to be lightly discounted—there's absolutely no pecking order among them, let alone an inflexible and unalterable one. The situation in England sometimes suggests, at least to an outsider, that the difference between Oxbridge and Redbrick is rather greater than the difference between Redbrick and no university education at all. In Germany, it doesn't matter where one studies; as long as one stays the course who graduates as a *Deutsche Akademiker* —for what that's worth nowadays, in the eyes of a wider world. (Leonhardt, 1964, 82)

Two aspects made the *abitur* (or secondary school leaving examination) especially appealing. Firstly, mathematics was a compulsory subject. This meant that every child in the gymnasium up to the age of nineteen was forced to take it, whether he or she was in a *Neusprachliches Gymnasium* (or modern language type school), or *Altsprachliches Gymnasium* (or classical type school), or (naturally enough) a *Mathmatisch-Naturwissenschaftliches Gymnasium*. Secondly, it is an internal examination, set and marked by teachers with the marked scripts moderated by an examining board. As such it appealed to many English educationists as a compromise between scholastic aptitude tests (as recommended by the Robbins Committee) and the existing type A-Levels (as set by the University Boards). One H.M.I. went so far as to say of the *abitur* that it was

> calculated to give the pupil a sense of security in a humanized examination in which his personality, his history, his record are taken into account by people with long-standing personal relationship. From the British point of view it is tantalizingly impressive that a modern, complex, industrialized society contrives

to serve its essential purpose—academic, technological, industrial, scientific—with one examination throughout its secondary education, and that an internal one at the age of 19. (Chapman, 1966, 309)

Signs of this admiration were seen in the Schools Council recommendation of 1967 for four subjects to be set and marked in the school, itself as 'electives' supporting two A-levels, and in the Dainton Report of 1968 suggesting that mathematics should become one of four compulsory A-level subjects in England, a suggestion echoed in modified form by Sir William Alexander.

The second: the East German Republic

With twice as many university students per head of the population and spending proportionately twice as much on education as West Germany, East Germany makes its Western counterpart look virtually class-ridden. Formed as the German Democratic Republic in October 1947 from the provinces of Old Prussia, Saxony, Saxon-Anhalt, Thuringia and Mecklenburg it has made education 'big business' (Hangen, 1967, 214). Polytechnically oriented, as in Russia, students work for one of their eleven terms in their future profession. Nearly all (some ninety-five per cent) are financed by the state.

Whereas West Germany has a school leaving age of fifteen, East Germany, since 1964, has raised it to sixteen, with the last three years focusing ever more sharply on the particular technology they will practise or need. Children work for one day a week or one week in three in a factory or on a farm. Clever ones are obliged to help their less fortunate contemporaries. Teachers are made personally responsible for seeing that the percentage of these less fortunate pupils leaving school early, does not rise above fifteen per cent. The whole youth world is wrapped, as in Russia, in the counterpart versions of the Pioneers and the Komsomol: the Thaelmann Pioneers and the Free German Youth (F.D.J.).

Such tight programming of East Germany's manpower is needed. Having lost four millions to the West since 1950, and having only seventeen to West Germany's fifty-eight million people, as well as having the fourth lowest birthrate in the world, it has yet managed to become, after the Soviet Union, West Germany, Britain and France, the fifth industrial power of Europe.

Their mutual technocratic base

The wall which at present divides the second and the fifth industrial powers of Europe cannot hide the technocratic élan which is stirring on both sides. For the managerial, Wellsian technocracy that George Orwell detected under Hitler has developed, though without the purges and concentration camps. Orwell, it will be remembered, wrote in 1941 that 'much of what Wells has imagined and worked for is physically there in Nazi Germany. The order, the planning, the State encouragement of science, the steel, the concrete, the aeroplanes are all there, but all in the service of ideas appropriate to the Stone Age' (Orwell, 1961, 164). The same pattern is emerging under Drs. Adenauer and Erhart and is emerging under Dr. Ulbricht but in the service of ideas appropriate to the twentieth century.

For though Adenauer symbolized the continuity with Weimar, when he had, as mayor, ringed Cologne with a green belt by buying up the military land round the city, converting the forts to pavilions for the playing fields, and capping it with a huge stadium, he also realized the need to employ good managers, whether Nazis or not (Montgomery, 1957, 120).

One can see the technocratic spirit of West Germany embodied in the activities of Professor Hallstein, the head of the German delegation to the Schumann Plan (from which the European Coal and Steel Community took shape), and co-signatory of the Rome Treaties (which set up E.E.C. and Euratom). Appointed first President of the E.E.C. Commission in January 1958 he worked to transform it into a United States of Europe. This has led to the merging of the Commission of E.E.C. and of Euratom, with the High Authority of E.C.S.C. As the voice of 'Eurocrats' he has, however, encountered difficulties from those who, like General de Gaulle, believe in a Europe *des patries*.

Of the 6,000 *fonctionnaires* who staff the European Community, 90 per cent speak French which, with German, forms the working language. Hallstein and other German technocrats were able to secure, in 1960–1, the conversion of O.E.E.C. (the Organization for European Economic Co-operation, the eighteen-nation agency for distributing American post-war help) into the O.E.C.D. (Organization for Economic Co-operation and Development). This new organization extended its co-operative activities to helping developing countries and associated America and Canada with them in such enterprises. Hallstein later said 'These Britons should learn that they can no longer run the continent. Germany and France are the leaders of the continent' (Hiscocks, 1966, 237).

The East German embodiment of the late twentieth-century technocrat was Dr. Erich Apel, an engineer, who, though not a member of the East German Communist Party till 1957, became Minister of Heavy Machine Building. He committed suicide on 3 December 1965 because of Russian demands for the prosperous hive he and other technocrats were helping to build. 'The fact is' wrote Welles Hangen 'that Erich Apel was not unique. Some of his fellow technocrats have already attained positions of importance; others are waiting impatiently to inherit power' (Hangen, 1967, 9). Certainly the 'pivotal position occupied by the industrial managers' (ibid, 88) justifies Hangen's claim that East Germany's 'new economic system is one of the most revolutionary experiments in the communist world since de-Stalinization' (ibid, 89). Certainly the fact that its growth rate by 1965 equalled that of West Germany's seven per cent is another indication that tradition dies hard. East Germany, as well as their sundered brothers in the West, are still setting a fast economic pace. That pace in the West is set by the industrial hierarchy. For 60 per cent of their firms employ one or more qualified scientists, engineers, and managers as opposed to Britain, where only 30 per cent do so. Commenting on this disparity the president of the Royal Society suggested that it was imposed on Britain not only by the structure of industry (too many small firms) but also by 'the deficiencies of our educational system' (*The Times Business News*, 21 February 1968, p. 19).

Ostpolitik and its consequences

As West Germany began to look eastwards for markets, sending diplomats and industrialists to Rumania, Hungary, and Czechoslovakia on trade missions, the U.S.S.R. became suspicious and took steps to block such economic penetration. In the case of Czechoslovakia those steps resulted in the occupation of the country by Soviet troops in 1968.

This has, if anything, strengthened German desire for a European confederation; especially for a confederation including Britain, Ireland and Scandinavia. Indeed this desire at the time of writing is so great that some Germans would be prepared to go ahead with this project omitting France altogether.

11

Conclusion:
The Missioners of knowledge

The technology of transmitting knowledge

Since the etymology of writing and books stems from the germanic verb meaning 'to scratch' and the German noun for a beech tree, it is fitting that Germans should have also contributed so much to the technology of diffusing knowledge in England.

Since the art of printing from wood blocks was rediscovered by Gütenberg at Mainz, (who invented a press for printing sheets on both sides in 1445), the Germans and the Dutch set a fast pace in the production of books. Though the cylinder for printing (instead of a flat plate) was first suggested by an Englishman (William Nicholson), it was a German (Koenig) who first devised its use with steam power in 1811. This was developed in Bolt Court London by another German (Bauer) and used by *The Times* in 1814 to produce 1,100 impressions an hour.

Visual illustration also owed much to them. Early German woodcutters, like Dürer, are well known. Lithography, the process by which a block of limestone can be used to print pictures by protecting the firm outline of the original drawing by surrounding it with gum arabic, was discovered by Senefelder in 1796. The subsequent substitution of limestone by zinc (in 1885) and aluminium (in 1890) and of gum arabic by gelatine and albumen were also of continental (or American) origin. So too was photogravure, the process which made possible the illustrated magazine, which was devised by Karl Klic in 1880, on the basis of previous work elsewhere.

The first press at Cambridge was set up by John Siberch of Cologne in 1521 in the face of ecclesiastical opposition. So too one of the earliest mass publishers was H. G. Bohn, son of a German who married the steam-engine pioneer's niece, Elizabeth Watt.

When Napoleon ravaged the continent, Bohn's father virtually picked up the books hastily sold before his arrival. H. G. Bohn himself professed to concentrate on issuing cheap but elegantly printed books, some 600 titles in all. Emerson said he had done as much for literature as railroads had done for international intercourse and Gladstone is said to have offered him a baronetcy. His apprentice, also a German, Bernhard Quaritch, became the leading antiquarian bookseller in Europe, renowned as the 'discoverer' of Omar Khayyám.

The very firm which published this book you are reading incorporated the firm of another German publisher, that of Nicholas Trübner. It was in his firm that William Heinemann learned his trade. Certainly the example of the German firm of Springer in Berlin stimulated a number of English firms to undertake more imaginative technical imprints.

Enrichers of the provinces

As agents of local enlightenment, individual Germans have made great contributions to English provincial life. Thus in Manchester, Charles Frederick Brandt, fustian manufacturer, was active in the Manchester Literary and Philosophical Society since 1783. Nathan Mayer Rothschild arrived in Manchester in 1798, made a fortune as a cotton merchant and left in the year of Trafalgar for London. But the real influx came with the German

H

Jews who arrived after 1820 and settled in Manchester: Albrecht, Behrens, Frank, Liebert, Magnus, Mendel, Nathan, Reissard, Schwabe, all names of moment in that community (Frangopulo, 1962, 114). German firms in Manchester increased from nine to eighty in the first thirty-eight years of the century (Frangopulo, 1965, 192). An Anglo-German High School was opened at Manchester, and an Anglo-German School at Bowden.

To Manchester, after the German revolution of 1848, a thirty year old Westphalian was invited by Hermann Leo, a Lancashire calico printer. There, with the support of German and other foreign business men, he began a series of concerts in the Free Trade Hall in 1858. This was the beginning of the oldest orchestra in Britain and the fourth oldest in the world—it is still called by the emigré's name: The Halle Orchestra.

Later contributions of German Jews like Behrens and Moser to the textile trade of Bradford or like Ludwig Mond to the chemical industry of South Lancashire, of Edgar Speyer and Ernest Cassell to the metropolitan banking world need mention since they were particularly generous donors or participators in the cultural life of their areas, and did not canton out for themselves a separate cultural life of their own.

Two Germans who did much for the education and medical aid of the poor in Manchester were the Rev. Joseph Steinthal (pastor of the German Mission Church in John Dalton Street) and his friend Dr. Louis Borchardt who developed the General Hospital and Dispensary for Sick Children at Pendlebury. Then there were the Salis-Schwabes: the husband raised money for a hospital for the insane, and the wife founded the Froebel Institute.

Froebelianism itself was imported by Germans, as we shall now see.

Froebelianism and the Ronges

Froebelianism was linked to advanced religious as well

as educational ideas, and one of its earliest practitioners in England were Johannes and Bertha Ronge. Johannes was described by the *Christian World* of 3 November 1887 as 'A Dangerous Reformer', because in a chapel annexed to his home in Tavistock Place, with a ceiling decorated with a plan of the solar system, he preached a pantheistic gospel unendorsed by priests or politicians.

For Ronge, exiled after the German disturbances of 1848, was a Froebelian who believed with Froebel that development must come from within, and so freed his children for games and creative work. Froebelian games and creative work in the kindergarten (the word was his own) enabled a child to explore Nature and so find God. Such ideas were not popular so his schools were closed by the Prussian Government.

Nor is it surprising for Froebelian ideas were particularly dear to progressive humanitarians with reforming sympathies anxious to enlist parental rather than priestly support in running schools. Johannes and Bertha Ronge were just such a couple and on their arrival in England they set up a kindergarten—first in Hampstead, then at 32 Tavistock Place, St. Pancras. Their school was linked to a kind of ethical church and had a senior department known as Humanistic Schools.

Visiting the Manchester exiles, the Ronges won several converts and established the Manchester Committee for the Kindergarten System in 1857 and a Manchester Froebel Society in 1873.

Another apostle of Froebel was the articulate, charming, multi-lingual Baroness von Bulow, who secured entry at the highest level in most European countries, and support from numerous men of repute.

At an Educational Exhibition in 1854 organized by the Royal Society of Arts, Bertha Ronge first exhibited the work of nursery children and the famous Froebel objects. Her book *Practical Guide to the English Kindergarten* (1855) went to fourteen editions in 30 years. The exhibition was followed by the arrival of the Baroness who also issued a book: *Woman's Educational Mission, Being an Explanation of Friedrich Froebel's System of Infant Gardens.* 'Infant Gardens': one of the first English assessments of Froebel, appeared in *Household Words* of 21 July, 1855, and was written by Henry Morley, later a professor at University College, London. This was the prelude to its ideas being adopted, as most people thought the article was written by Charles Dickens. They were the subject of lectures at the polytechnic and an H.M.I., the Rev. M. Mitchell, hailed them with enthusiasm. Taken up by the Mayo's Home and Colonial Society in 1859, endorsed by the Newcastle Commission in 1861, and adopted by the British and Foreign Schools Society in 1865, Froebelian ideas found their three major women expositors in Eleanora Heerwort, Madame Michelis and Miss Caroline Bishop, who joined forces with the first professor of education in Britain, Joseph Payne, to form the Froebel Society in 1874. Two years later this began to give certificates of proficiency and by 1887 became the National Froebel Union.

Like Herbartianism, Froebelianism was touted as a German nostrum—notably by educationists like H. T. Mark, whose *Education and 'Efficiency' An Application of some of Froebel's ideas to English Education* (1904) shows the winds that were blowing such doctrines to England.

Science and Charles Reiner

Another exile, Charles Reiner, contributed much to science teaching by basing its teaching on the experience of the child. He came to England from Yverdun to propagate Pestalozzian ideas through the Home and Colonial Infant School Society. This body was formed in 1836 by an enthusiastic Anglican clergyman who believed that by using objects of everyday life as the basis for lessons in the classroom, that children's perceptions and ideas could be enriched. Certainly as practised by Reiner in the teaching of mathematics and chemistry (on which he wrote books), the object lesson rose above mere moralism and established itself as a viable standard technique in English schools up to the present time. This basic Pestalozzian technique was to win numerous other English admirers, most notably Dr. James-Kay Shuttleworth who cast over it the mantle of official sponsorship.

One of his pupils, Dean Fremantle, described Reiner as 'without exception the best teacher I have ever known, both for his knowledge and his method and his discipline. He never set a punishment and was rarely disobeyed. A nation ruled as he ruled us would have few rebellious subjects'. For Reiner taught up till 1849 at a school that since his time has become famous: Cheam. Here he had other distinguished pupils too—including Hugh Childers, a Liberal Chancellor of the Exchequer, who acknowledged that his own mastery of mathematics came from Reiner's 'activity' methods and his habit of inviting foreign lecturers, like Professor Schonbein, to experiment before them. Childers was inspired to make models in the vacations—one of Vesuvius, actually smoked and erupted lava.

Two recent historians of the school have acknowledged that much of its merit came from Reiner's teaching of science, describing him as 'a subtler Pestalozzian and more brilliant teacher than Mayo,' who 'gave to the school an unusual and unremarked distinction—that of an excellent institution for the teaching of science' (Stewart and McCann, 1967, 178). Nor in the later diffusion of Pestalozzian ideas, should the work of W. H. Herford be ignored. He established in Manchester the Lady Barn House School in 1873, and for its first ten years, over a third of its pupils were of German origin (Hicks, 1936, p. 35).

Alienation and Karl Marx

Nineteenth-century émigrés were 'more numerous and

more quarrelsome than those of other nationalities', and, by keeping aloof from the others, they reflected 'the absence of unity which disfigured Germany itself' (Carr, 1934, 140–1). One can see this in the 'St. John's Wood Set' in which the leading light was a handsome talented poet, who had escaped from Spandau gaol to England in 1850. Here he tried to raise money for a future German republic. His impetuosity outraged another refugee, who shunned him and his set: Karl Marx.

Marx was attracted to the most permanent of these groups, the German Workers' Educational Union. He was introduced to it by his friend Engels and when he returned to settle permanently in London, first at Camberwell, then at Dean Street, Soho, then Haverstock Hill, then at Maitland Park, he used it as a kind of club. Between Marx in London and Engels in Manchester shuttled a correspondence illuminating the great events of the century, round which a literature of commentary and exegesis has exfoliated.

Moreover the German Workers' Educational Union went from strength to strength. It took, under J. G. Eccarius, a leading rôle in the establishment of the first Internationale and by 1885 was the strongest of all existing German organizations in London. Several of its members were German schoolmasters. Nor should we forget that it was to the memory of a Silesian school teacher that Marx dedicated *Das Kapital* (1867).

Child Therapy and Anna Freud

Marx held that some men were 'alienated' from their work and the products of such work by the social (and class) system, which led to alienation from their own true nature. (Marx, 1959, 67–84). This idea was developed still further by Freud who was one of some 8,000 exiles who came to England after 1932 when Hitler exiled the Jews. With him came his daughter Anna, in 1938. Whereas he charted adult anxieties, she charted those of children. She

trained as a teacher, and became the first child psycho-
therapist. Her book on child analysis, published in 1927,
is now known all over the world. In 1936 she described
children's reactions to external and internal dangers.
These dangers multiplied a year after she arrived in England, when the war, with the enormous dislocation of
family lives, presented her with the opportunity of starting a child nursery in Hampstead to care for the childhood victims. This was so successful that in 1951 it was
reorganized as the Hampstead Child Therapy Clinic.

Here Anna Freud's growing and devoted team has
been treating children for whom blindness, or deafness or
being orphaned early in life has beset them with problems.
Fifteen years of careful clinical observations have given
us a clearer understanding of the psychic contours of
these childhood victims of Nature and Fate, so that we can
now entertain surer expectations of their potential in
terms of accomplishments, conflicts and difficulties. These
surer expectations are embodied in the famous Hampstead Index, now a study in its own right. That this is so
is due to it being based on clinical observation and practice, with theory properly used to unlock closed doors
before exploration begins inside. These direct observations of children are shared by her fellow analysts, and
brought into focus by weekly discussions and teamwork.

Educational planning

Other exiled Germans of the 1930's have made a major
contribution to English higher education.

Physicists like Born and Simon, chemists like Polanyi,
biochemists like Krebs and Friedmann, physiologists like
Hotega and psychiatrists like Freud stimulated their fields.
So did the transfer from Hamburg to London of the
Warburg Institute of the History of Thought and Art.

Educational thought in particular was especially enriched by the personality of Karl Mannheim (a notable
sociologist at the University of Heidelberg) who main-

tained that the intellectual, being classless, could either place himself at the disposal of a class to formulate ideas congenial to it, or could mediate between classes and so synthesize ideas for society. Mannheim himself fell into the second category, and his synthesis of ideas centred the need to 'plan for life'.

> Such planning [he wrote] is a very important element of the rationalization of man, as more than anything else it keeps the individual from yielding to momentary impulses (Momentreacktionen). Its destruction increases to an extraordinary degree the suggestibility of the individual and strengthens the belief in miraculous cure-alls. (Kotschnig, 1937, 177)

Planning cadres, he thought, would need to be intelligent, so he argued for the selection of an élite through objective tests.

Mannheim's impact on educational thought in the early period of post-war planning is reflected in the writings of Sir Fred Clarke, the first chairman of the National Advisory Council on Education; and in the polemical tract of T. S. Eliot: *Notes towards the Definition of Culture* (1948). For he helped many to see the necessity of democratic planning to ensure the maintenance of freedom: a lesson which German exiles, above all, had learned the hard way, and which we in England are now following.

Mannheim was the last and perhaps one of the most effective German exponents of the need for planning in England, tempering the arguments of a long line of his fellow countrymen who ever since the time of List had been forging arguments for a welfare-warfare state. For it was the warfare rather than the welfare aspect of German education that had excited English observers before his time. A British army chaplain noted this but attributed it to Catholicism. (Taylor, 1745). Others, like the shrewd Scottish kelp-trader, Samuel Laing, described German education as

a deception practised for the paltry political end of

rearing the individual to be part and parcel of a despotic system of government; of training him to be either its instrument or its slave, according to his social station. (Laing, 1842, 94)

Even such well-disposed Americans as Horace Mann noted 'the quiescence or torpidity of social life' which 'stifles the activity excited in the schoolroom'. He saw 'the power of the goverment' pressing 'upon the partially developed faculties of youth as with a mountain's weight' (Mann, 1846, 200).

Mark Pattison went further, detecting a development from 'docility in the child' into 'stupidity, submissiveness, and a mechanical routine existence.... No one around him thinks of acquiring information except in his own pursuit (*fach*)'. (Pattison, 1861, 243).

An Anglo-American noted that 'German normal schools illustrate the danger of applying bureaucratic methods in education' (Kandel, 1910, 126); whilst even the hospitable dons who gave refuge to the exiled German professors at Oxford in the 1930's noticed how they exhaled the manner of sergeant-majors (Bowra, 1967, 302).

Émigrés speak English

'You can at any time learn ffrench in a Week.... Not so the German I fear I shall never be the master of it' (Morley, 1929, 58). Crabb Robinson's confession to his brother on 11 February, 1801 was echoed by Gilbert and Sullivan in 1895 when in *The Grand Duke* (1895) Julia complained 'Ach what a crackjaw language this German is'.

Such complaints were common, even amongst university teachers in the last century. After taking up German and 'fretting over the thing for a dozen years', constantly reminding himself of the importance of being able to read 'the useful books' ... in theology, Cardinal Newman finally had to give it up. (Culler, 1955, 47). Even more surprisingly, that epitome of scholarship, Mark

Pattison, complained that the task of coping with the German declension was 'despairing'.

Transcending these linguisitic barriers, émigrés like Mannheim enabled Englishmen 'to catch up with German philosophy' a task estimated as taking about half a century (Kauffman, 1960, 258). Hence the reason (as I have indicated in a previous volume in this series) for many German educational ideas coming to this country via America, partly because Americans were anxious to assimilate the best of European practice, partly because a number of Germans emigrated there (Munroe, 1907). Yet though America has been virtually a relay station for German ideas, even they had difficulties with the language, as Mark Twain indicated when he confessed that his own philological studies had convinced him that 'a gifted person ought to learn English (barring spelling and pronouncing) in thirty hours, French in thirty days, and German in thirty years.'

Bibliography

Association of Jewish Refugees in Great Britain, *Britain's New Citizens, The Story of the Refugees from Germany and Austria*, (A. J. R., 8, Fairfax Mansions, Finchley Road, London, 1952).

A Member of the Inner Temple, *The University of Bonn. Its Rise, Progress and Present State*, London : 1845, 19.

ADAM, REV. JAMES, *The Prussian System of Popular and National Education, its history, character and prospects*, Edinburgh : John Johnstone, 1846.

ADAMS, HENRY, *The Education of Henry Adams: An Autobiography*, London : Constable and Co., 1928.

ADAMS, JOHN, *The Herbartian Psychology as applied to Education*, London : Isbister and Co., 1897.

ALTHAUS, F., 'Beiträge zur Geschichte der deutschen Colonie in England', *Unsere Zeit Deutsche Revue der Gegenwort*, N. F., 9 Jahrang, Erste Hälfte, Leipsig, 1873, 433-445, 534-548.

ANDERSON, P., *The Background of Anti-English feeling in Germany 1890–1902*, American University Press : Washington, 1939.

ARMYTAGE, W. H. G., *A. J. Mundella 1825–1897. The Liberal Background of the Labour Movement*, London : Ernest Benn, 1951.

ARMYTAGE, W. H. G., *The Rise of the Technocrats*, London : Routledge & Kegan Paul, 1965.

ARNOLD, ARMIN, *Heine in England and America*, London : Linden Press, 1959.

ARNOLD, MATTHEW, *Higher Schools and Universities in Germany*, London : Macmillan and Co., 1874.

ASHLEY, SIR WILLIAM, *The Tariff Problem*, London : P. S. King and Son, 1903.

ASHLEY, W. J., *The Progress of the German Working Classes during the last Quarter of a Century*, London : Longmans & Co., 1904.

AUDEN, W. H., *The Wandering Jew*, New York : New Republic, 1941, 11, 186.

AUSTIN, SARAH, See Cousin, V.

BANFIELD, T. G., *Industry of the Rhine*, London : Charles Knight, 1846.

BARGER, FLORENCE, E., *Continuation School Work in the Grand Duchy of Baden and in Canton Zurich*, Educational Pamphlet No. 6, Board of Education, London: H.M.S.O., 1907.

BACHE, A. D., *Report on Education in Europe to the Trustees of Girard College*, Philadelphia: Girard College, 1839.

BARKER, J. ELLIS, *Modern Germany*, London: Smith Elder, 1912, 4th edition.

BARKER, J. ELLIS, 'The Future of Anglo-German Relations', *Nineteenth Century*, 1906.

BARTHOLOMEW, A. T., *A Bibliography of A. W. Ward*, Cambridge: University Press, 1926.

BEARD, J. R. (Ed.), *Voices of the Church in Reply, to Dr. D. F. Strauss*, London: Simpkin, Marshall & Co., 1845.

BEATTIE, JOHN M., *The English Court in The Reign of George I*, London: Cambridge Press, 1967.

BEATTIE, WILLIAM, *Life and Letters of Thomas Campbell*, London: Edward Moxon, 1850, ii, 366.

BECKER, JOSEF., *Von der Bauakademie zur Technischen Universität*, Berlin-Wilmersdorf: O. H. O. Hellwig & Co., 1949.

BECKMANN, J. J., *A History of Inventions and Discoveries*, translated by William Johnston, London: J. Bell, 1797. [This was later, 1846, published in Bohn's Standard Library.]

BENTWICH, NORMAN, *The Refugees from Germany*, London: George Allen and Unwin, 1936.

BERNHARDI, F. VON, *Germany and the Next War 1911*, translated Allen H. Powles, London: Edward Arnold, 1914.

BEST, R. H., *The Brassworkers of Berlin and Birmingham. A Comparison. Joint Report of R. H. Best, L. T. Davis and C. Perks*, London: P. S. King, 1905, 3rd Edition; 1910, 5th edition.

BEST, R. H. and OGDEN, C. K., *The Problem of Continuation Schools and its Successful Solution in Germany, with an introduction by Dr. Georg Kerschensteiner*, London: P. S. King and Son, 1914.

BIRD, CHARLES B. A., *Higher Education in Germany and England; being a brief practical account of the organisation and curriculum of the German Higher Schools with critical remarks and suggestions with reference to those of England.* London: Kegan Paul & Co., 1884.

BLACKIE, J. S., 'The Importance of the German Language and reasons for its more general cultivation in this country', *Edinburgh Literary Journal Miscellany*, 2, 1829, 163.

BLATTNER, FRITZ, *Das Gymnasium*, Heidelberg: Quelle and Meyer, 1960.

BLUHM, R. K., 'Henry Oldenburg, F.R.S.', *Notes and Records of the Royal Society*, xv, 1960, 183–197.

BOARD OF EDUCATION, *Interim Report of the Consultative Committee on Scholarships* on *Higher Education*, London: H.M.S.O. Cmnd. 8291, 1916.

BONNER, THOMAS, N., *American Doctors and German Universities*, Lincoln: 1963.

BOOTH, MEYRICK, 'The German Youth Movement', *Hibbert Journal*, xxii, 1923, 468–478.

BOWRA, C. M., *Memories 1898–1939*, London: Weidenfeld and Nicolson, 1966.

BOWRING, JOHN, *Report on the Prussian Commerical Union*, London: H.M.S.O. Parliamentary Papers XXI, 1840.

BRAVER, G., *Die hannoveresch-englischen Subsidienverträge, 1702–48*, Aachen, 1962.

BRINKMANN, C., 'The Hanseatic League: A Survey of Recent History', *Journal of Economic and Business History*, ii (1929–30), 585–602.

BROOKS, R. A. E. (Ed.) *Carlyle's Journey to Germany Autumn 1858*, New Haven: Yale University Press, 1940.

BRUFORD, W. H., *Germany in the Eighteenth Century: The Social Background of the Literary Revival*, Cambridge: Univeristy Press, 1965.

BUCHNER, E. F., *The Educational Theory of Immanuel Kant*, London: J. B. Lippencott Company, 1908.

BURROW, J. W., 'The uses of Philology in Victorian England' in Robson, R. (Ed.), *Ideas and Institutions of Victorian Britain*, London: G. Bell and Sons, 1967.

BUTLER, E. M., *The Tyranny of Greece over Germany*, Cambridge University Press, 1938.

CAIRNS, JOHN, *Unbelief in the Eighteenth Century*, Edinburgh: Adam and Charles Black, 1881.

CAMERON, RONDO E., *France and the Economic Development of Europe*, Princeton, New Jersey: Princeton University Press, 1961.

CANNON, W. F., 'Scientists and Broad Churchmen: an Early Victorian Intellectual Network', *Journal of British Studies*, IV, 1964.

CARLYLE, THOMAS, *Critical and Miscellaneous Essays*, London: Chapman and Hall, 1869.

CARLYLE, THOMAS, *Early Letters*, ed. C. E. Norton, London: Macmillan, 1886.

CARLYLE, THOMAS, *Frederick the Great*, New York: Alden, 1885.

CARR, E. H., *Karl Marx. A Study of Fanaticism*, London: J. M. Dent and Sons, 1934.

CARR, G. T., 'Early German Grammars in England', *Journal of English and Germanic Philology*, 1937.

CARRE, J. M., *Goethe en Angleterre*, Paris: 1920.

CAZAMIAN, LOUIS, *Carlyle*, trans., by E. K. Brown, New York: Macmillan and Co., 1932.

CHAPMAN, COLIN, 'The A-Level Rat-Race', *New Statesman*, 2 September 1966, 309.

CHARLTON, H. B., *Portrait of a University*, Manchester: University Press, 1951.

CLARK, G. N., 'Origin of the Cambridge Modern History', *Cambridge Historical Journal*, viii, 1945, 57–64.

CLARKE, I. F., *Voices prophesying War*, 1763–1984, London: O.U.P., 1966.

CLARKE, M. L., *Richard Porson: A Biographical Essay*, Cambridge: University Press, 1937.

CLAY, H. A., *Compulsory Continuation Schools in Germany*, London, H.M.S.O. Educational Pamphlets No. 18, 1910.

COATS, R. H., *In Memoriam Robert Hall Best*, Birmingham: Kynoch Press, 1925.

COBURN, OLIVER, *Youth Hostel Story*, London: National Council of Social Service, 1950.

COLLINS, PHILIP, *Dickens and Education*, London: Macmillan and Co., 1963. 'A Note on Dickens and Froebel', *National Froebel Foundation Bulletin*, No. 94, 1955, 15–18.

CONRAD, J., *The German Universities for the past Fifty Years*, translated by John Hutchison and a preface by James Bryce, Glasgow: David Bryce and Son, 1885.

CORDASCO, FRANCESCO G. M., *The Bohn Libraries. A History and a checklist*, New York: Burt Franklin Bibliographical Series No. 5, 1951.

COUSIN, V., *Report on the State of Public Instruction in Prussia*, translated by Sarah Austin, London: 1834.

COX, G. V., *Reminiscences of Oxford*, London: 1870.

DAINTON REPORT: *Enquiry into the Flow of Candidates in Science and Technology into Higher Education*, Cmnd. 3541, London: H.M.S.O., 1968.

DALE, F. H., 'Continuation Schools in Saxony', *Special Reports on Educational Subjects*, London: Eyre and Spottiswoode, vol. I, 1897.

DAWSON, W. H., *The Evolution of Modern Germany*, London: T. Fisher-Unwin (one of many books he wrote on this theme), 1908.

DAWSON, W. H., *School Doctors in Germany*, London: H.M.S.O. Educational Pamphlets No. 4, 1908.

DE HOVRE, FR., *German and English Education Compared*, London: Constable, 1917.

DEMETIZ, WILLIAM, 'Kafka in England', *German Life and Letters*, N.S., iv, 1950–1, 21–30.

DEUTSCH, KARL W. and EDINGER, LEWIS J., *Germany Rejoins the Powers*, Stanford University Press, 1959.

DOCKHORN, KLAUS, *Der deutsche Historismus in England*, Hesperia Ergänzungsheft 14, Göttingen: Vandenhoeck & Ruprecht, 1950.

DOCKHORN, KLAUS, *Deutscher Geist und Angelsächsische Geistesgeschichte*, Göttingen, Göttingen Bausteine zur Geschictswissenschaft, Band, 17, 1954.

DODD, CATHERINE, I., *Introduction to the Herbart's Principles of Teaching*, London: Swan Sonnenschein and Co., 1898.

DONALD, M. B., *Elizabethan Copper: The History of the Company of Mines Royal 1568–1605*, London: Pergamon Press, 1955.

DONALD, M. B., *Elizabethan Monopolies: The History of the Company of Mineral and Battery Works from 1565 to 1604*, Edinburgh: Oliver and Boyd, 1961.

DUFLOU, G., *L'Université d'Oxford et son Enseignement des Langues Modernes*, Ghent, 1894.

DUNSTAN., A. C., 'The German Influence on Coleridge', in: *Modern Languages Review 17* (1922) and *18* (1923).

EDINGER, LEWIS J., *German Exile Politics: The Social Democratic Executive Committee in the Nazi Era*, Berkeley: University of California, 1958.

ELLWEIN, THOMAS, *Das Regierungssystern der Bundes republik Deutschland*, Cologne: Westdeutscher Verlag, 1963.

FELKIN, H. M., *Technical Education in a Saxon Town*, London: Kegan Paul & Co., 1881.

FELKIN, H. M., and E. (ed.), *Herbart's Letters and Lectures on Education*, London: Swan Sonnenschein, 1898.

FICHT, GEORGE, *Die deutsche Bildungskatastrophe*, Freiburg: Walter-Verlag, 1964.

FIELDER, HERMA, 'German Musicians in England and their influence in the Era of the eighteenth century', *German Life and Letters*, 1939, iv, 1–15.

FINDLAY, J. J., 'The Genesis of the German Clerk', *Fortnightly Review*, 1899.

First Report of the Royal Commission on Technical Instruction, 1882.

FISCHER, W., *Deutsche Kultureinfluss am Victorianischen Hofe Giessener Beitrage 97*, Geissen: 1951.

FLETCHER, ARTHUR W., *Education in Germany*, Cambridge: W. Heffer and Sons, 1934.

FLEXNER, ABRAHAM, *Universities, American, English, German*, Oxford: University Press, 1930.

FORBES, DUNCAN, *The Liberal-Anglican Idea of History*, Cambridge, University Press, 1950.

FORSTER, 'G. R. Weckherlin in England', *German Life and Letters*, 3, 1938–9, 107–117.

FORSTER, LEONARD, 'John Disney and the Study of German in Early Eighteenth Century England', *German Life and Letters*, N.S. 16, 1962–3, 186–197.

FRANGOPULO, N. J., (Ed.), *Rich Inheritance: a Guide to the History of Manchester*, Manchester Education Committee, 1962.

FRANGOPULO, N. J., 'Foreign Communities in Victorian Manchester', *Manchester Review*, X (1965), 189–206.

FREEMANTLE, FRANCES, *A Traveller's Study of Health and Empire*, London: John Ouseley, 1911.

FRIEDRICH, E., *Die Entwicklung des Realienunterrichtes bis zu den ersten Realschulgründungen*, Weida, 1913.

GAG, WANDA, *Tales from Grimm*, and *More Tales from Grimm*, London: Faber, 1937 and 1962.

GARDNER, PERCY, *Oxford at the Cross Roads*, London: A. and C. Black, 1903.

GARDINER, H. R., *World Without End. British Politics and the Younger Generation*, London: Cobden-Sanderson, 1932.

GARDINER, (H.) ROLF, and ROCHOLL, HANS, *Britain and Germany: A Frank Discussion instigated by Members of the Younger Generation*, London: Williams and Morgate, 1928.

GARDINER, SAMUEL RAWSON, *Letters and other documents illustrating the relations between England and Germany at the commencement of the thirty years' war*, 2 vols., London, 1865.

GEEHL, H., *Deutschlands Pionere in London, Ein Wegweiser und Rathgeber für Deutsche in England*, Berlin: C. Janke, 1883.

GILLESPIE, C. C., *Geology and Genesis: A study in the relation of scientific thought, natural theology and social opinion in Great Britain 1790–1850*, Cambridge, Mass.: Harvard University Press, 1961. [Harvard Historical Studies, vol. 58.]

GIBB, F. W., 'Invention in Chemical Industries' in SINGER, CHARLES, HOLMYARD, E. J., HALL, A. R. and WILLIAMS, T. I. (ed.), *A History of Technology*, London: Oxford University Press, 1957, 676–708.

GILBERT, MARTIN, *The Roots of Appeasement*, London: Weidenfeld and Nicolson, 1966.

GOLDMANN, *Secretary of Europe! The Life of Fredrich Gentz Enemy of Napoleon*, New Haven: Yale University Press, 1948.

GOSTICK, JOSEPH, *German Culture and Christianity: Their Controversy in the Time 1770–1780* London: 1882.

GRAY, R. D., 'English Resistance to German Literature from Coleridge to D. H. Lawrence' in *The German Tradition in Literature 1871–1945*, Cambridge University Press, 1965.

GREEN, V. H. H., *Oxford Common Room*, London: Edward Arnold, 1957.

GREIG, J. Y. T., *Letters of David Hume*, Oxford: 1932.

HABER, L. F., *The Chemical Industry during the Nineteenth Century*, Oxford: Clarendon Press, 1958.

HAHN, KURT, 'Outward Bound', *The Year Book of Education*, London: Evan Brothers, 1957, 436–462.

HAILLE, H. G., *The History of Dr. Faustus*, Urbana: University of Illinois Press, 1965.

HAINES, IV, GEORGE, *German Influence upon English Education and Science 1800–1866*, New London: Connecticut College, 1957, LXXII.

HAINES IV, GEORGE, 'German Influence upon Scientific Instruction in England 1867–1887', *Victorian Studies*, 1 (1957–8), 1958, 213.

HANGEN, WELLES, *The Muted Revolution. East Germany's Challenge to Russia and the West*, London: Victor Gollancz, 1967.

HALDANE, R. B., *An Autobiography*, London: Hodder and Stoughton, 1929.

HALE, BELLOT, H., *University College, London 1826–1926*, London: University Press, 1929.

HALÉVY, ELIE, *Thomas Hodgskin* ed. in Translation by A. J. Taylor, London: Ernest Benn, 1956.

HAMILTON, HENRY, *The English Brass and Copper Industries to 1800*, London: Longmans & Co., 1926.

HANEY, J. L., *The German Influence on S. T. Coleridge*, Philadelphia: 1902.

HARRIS, W. J., *The First Printed Translations into English of the Great Foreign Classics*, London: Routledge, 1909 (V. incomplete).

HARROLD, C. F., *Carlyle and German Thought 1819–1834*, New Haven, Connecticut, Yale Studies in English, No. 82, 1934.

HASSE, A. C., *The United Brethren in England from 1641–1742*, London: W. Mallalieu, 1867.

HAUHART, WILLIAM FREDERICK, *The Reception of Goethe's Faust in England in the First Half of the Nineteenth Century*, New York: Columbia University Press, 1909.

HAYWARD, F. H., *An Educational Failure. A School Inspector's Story*, London: Duckworth, 1938.

HAYWARD, F. H., *The Student's Herbart: A Brief Educational Monograph dealing with the Movement by Herbart and developed by Stoy, Dörpfeld and Ziller*, London: Swan Sonnenschein and Co., 1902.

HAYWARD, F. H., and THOMAS, M. E., *The Critics of Herbartianism*, London: Swan Sonnenschein, 1903.

HEATH, SIR H. FRANK and HETHERINGTON, A. L., *Industrial Research and Development in the United Kingdom*, a survey, London: Faber and Faber, 1946.

HEATON, H., *The Yorkshire Woollen and Worsted Industries*, 2nd edn., Oxford: Clarendon Press, 1965.

HELMREICH, E. C., *Religious Education in German Schools. An Historical Approach*, Cambridge, Mass., Harvard University Press, 1959.

HENDERSON, W. O. and CHALLONER, W. H., 'Friedrich Engels in Manchester', *Memoirs and Proceedings of the Manchester Literary and Philosophical Society*, vol. 98.

HERFORD, C. H., *Studies in the Literary Relations of England and Germany in the Sixteenth Century*, Cambridge: University Press, 1886.

HICKS, W. C. R., *Lady Barn House and the work of W. H. Herford*, Manchester: University Press, 1936.

HICKS, W. C. R., *The School in English and German Fiction*, London: Soncino Press, 1933.

HIGGINSON, J. G., 'Sadler's German Studies', *British Journal of Educational Studies*, (1958).

HIMMELFARB, GERTRUD, *Lord Acton: A Study in Conscience and Politics*, London: Routledge and Kegan Paul, 1952.

HINTON, THOMAS R., 'German Intellectuals on the Eve of 1848', *German Life and Letters*, NS, 2, 1948–9, 13–21.

HISCOCKS, RICHARD, *Germany Revived, an Appraisal of the Adenauer Era*, London: Victor Gollancz, 1966.

HODGSKIN, T., *Travels in the North of Germany*, Edinburgh: Archibald Constable and Co., 1820.

HODGSON, W. B., (Ed.), *Report of an Educational Tour, being part of the Seventh Annual Report of Horace Mann 1844*, London: Simpkin, Marshall, and Company, 1846.

HÖCKER, WILMA, *Der Gesandte Bunsen als Vermittler zwischen Deutschland und England*, Göttingen: Munsterschmit, Wissenschaftlicher Verlag, 1951.

HOFFMAN, ROSS J. S., *Great Britain and the German Trade Rivalry 1875–1914*, New York: Russell and Russell, 1964.

HOGG, O. F. G., *The Royal Arsenal. Its Background, Origin and Subsequent History*, London: Oxford University Press, 1963.

HORN, DAVID BAYNE, *Great Britain and Europe in the Eighteenth Century*, Oxford: Clarendon Press, 1967.

HORSFALL CARTER, W., *Speaking European The Anglo-Continental Cleavage*, London: George Allen and Unwin, 1966.

HORSFALL, T. C., *Professor Rein's System of Religious Education for Schools*, a paper read to the Manchester-Rochdale Edn. Society, 20 Jan., 1905.

HORSFALL, T. C., *The Improvement of the Dwellings and Surroundings of the People—The Example of Germany*, Manchester: Citizens Association for the Improvement of the Dwellings of the People, 1904.

HORSFALL, T. C., *National Service and the Welfare of the Community*, intro. by Vivian Grey (E. E. Mills), London: Simpkin Marshall, 1906.

HOWARTH, O. J. R., *The British Association for the Advancement of Science. A Retrospect 1831–1931*, London: British Association, 1931.

HOWELL, JAMES, *Instructions for Forreine Travell*, London: 1869 (orig. ed. 1642), ed. Arber.

HOWITT, WILLIAM, *The Rural and Domestic Life of Germany*, London: Longman, Brown, Green and Longman, 1842.

HÜBENER, GUSTAV, 'The Present Mind of German Universities', *Hibbert Journal*, xxiii, 1924–5.

HÜBER, V. A., *The English Universities, an abridged translation by F. W. Newman*, London : W. Pickering, 1843.

HUEBENER, THEODORE, *The Schools of West Germany*, New York : University Press, 1962.

HUGHES, CHARLES, *Shakespeare's Europe*. Unpublished chapters of Fynes Moryson's Itinerary, Being a Survey of the Condition of Europe at the end of the 16th century . . . London : Sherratt and Hughes, 1903.

HUNT, MARGARET (Trans. aided) and STERN, JAMES, *Grimm's Fairy Tales*, London : Routledge, 1948.

HUNT, RICHARD N., *German Social Democracy 1918–1933*, New Haven, Conn. : Yale University Press, 1964.

HURLIMANN, BETTINA, *Three Centuries of Children's Books in Europe*, London : Oxford University Press, 1967.

HUTTON, J. E., *A History of the Moravian Church*, London: Moravian Publication Office, 1909.

HYLLA, E. J. and KEGEL, F. O., *Education in Germany*, Frankfurt-am-Main : Hochschule für Internationale Pädagogische Forschung, 1954.

In Northern Europe 1930: Activities by some Members of the Younger Generation in Britain and Germany, London: Anglo-German Academic Bureau, 1931.

JASPERS, KARL, *The Future of Germany*, London : University of Chicago Press, 1968.

JONES, T., *Lloyd George*, London: Oxford University Press, 1951.

KAHN, LUDWIG W., *Social Ideas in German Literature 1770–1830*, New York : Columbia Univ. Press 1938.

KANDEL, I. L., *The Training of Elementary School Teachers in Germany*, New York : Teachers' College, 1910.

KAUFFMANN, WALTER, *The Owl and the Nightingale from Shakespeare to Existentialism*, London : Faber and Faber, 1960.

KELLY, J. A., *German Visitors to English Theatres in the Eighteenth Century*, Princeton, New Jersey : University Press, 1936.

KELLY, J. A., *England and the Englishman in German Literature of the Eighteenth Century*, New York : Columbia University Press, 1921.

KELLNER, L., *Alexander von Humboldt*, London : Oxford University Press, 1963.

KENT, DONALD PETERSON, *The Refugee Intellectual. The*

Americanisation of the Immigrants of 1933–41, New York: Columbia University Press, 1953.

KIELMANSEGGE, F. VON, *Diary of a Journey to England (in the years 1761–62)*, London: Longmans & Co., 1902.

KLEMM, FREDERICH, *A History of Western Technology* (transl. Dorothea Waley Singer), London: George Allen and Unwin, 1959.

KLEMPERER, KLEMENS, VON, *Germany's New Conservatism: Its History and Dilemma in the Twentieth Century*, Princeton, New Jersey: Princeton University Press, 1957.

KLENZE, C. VON, 'German Predecessors of Ruskin', *Modern Philology*, 1906.

KOHLS, ERNST WILHELM, *Die Schule bei Martin Bucer*, Heidelberg: Quelle and Meyer, 1963.

KOHN, HANS, *The Mind of Germany. The Education of a Nation*, London: Macmillan, 1961.

KOTSCHNIG, WALTER M., *Unemployment in the Learned Professions*, London: Oxford University Press, 1937.

KOTSCHNIG, WALTER M. and PRYS, ELINER (ed.), *The University in a Changing World*, London: Humphrey Milford, 1932.

KUEHNEMUND, R., *Arminus or The Rise of a National Symbol in Literature*, Chapel Hill: University of North Carolina, 1953.

LAING, S., *Notes of a traveller on the social and political state of France, Prussia, Switzerland, Italy and other parts of Europe*, London: Longman, Brown, Green & Longmans, 1854.

LAQUER, WALTER Z., *Young Germany: A History of the German Youth Movement*, London: Routledge and Kegan Paul, 1962.

LASKI, N. J., 'The History of Manchester Jewry', *Manchester Review*, Summer 1956, 366–375.

LAUE, THEODORE VON, *Leopold Ranke*, Princeton, New Jersey: Princeton University Press, 1956.

LEARNED, W. S., *The Overlehrer; a study of the social and professional evolution of the German schoolmaster*, Cambridge: Harvard University Press, 1914.

LEONHARDT, R. W., 'In Lieu of Robbins', *Encounter*, xxii, April 1964, pp. 80–2.

LETTS, MALCOLM, *As the Foreigner saw us*, London: Methuen & Co., 1935.

LEXIS, WILHELM, *A General View of the History and Organisation of Public Education in the German Empire*, Berlin: A. Ascher and Co., 1904.

LIEBIG, JUSTUS VON, 'Der Zustand der chemie in Preussen', *Annalen der Chemie und Pharmacie*, xxxiv, 1840–47.

LILGE, FREDERIC, *The Abuse of Learning. The Failure of the German University*, New York: Macmillan and Co., 1948.

LINDEGREN, ALINE M., *Education in Germany*, Bulletin No. 15, 1938, Washington: Government Printing Office, 1939.

LINDEGREN, ALINE M., *Germany Revisted. Education in the German Federal Republic*, Washington: U.S. Office of Education, 1957, No. 12.

LINGELBACH, W. E., 'The Merchant Adventurers at Hamburg', *American Historical Review*, IX, 1903–4, 265–87.

LINSTEAD, SIR PATRICK, 'The Prince Consort F.R.S. and the founding of Imperial College', *Notes and Records of the Royal Society*, xvii, 1962, 15–31.

LIPSON, E., *The Economic History of England*, London: A. C. Black, 1961.

LIPTZIN, S., *The English Legend of Heinrich Heine*, New York: Bloch Publishing Co., 1954.

LUARD, EVAN, *The Cold War: A Reappraisal*, London: Thames and Hudson, 1964.

MAGALL, C. P., 'An English Liberal in Germany 1840–1842', *German Life and Letters*, 1937, 218–228.

MANN, HORACE, see HODGSON.

MANNHEIM, KARL, *Ideology and Utopia*, Bonn: 1929.

MANSEL, H. L., Phrontisterion, in *Letters and Reviews*, ed., Henry W. Chandler, London: J. Murray, 1873.

MARE, MARGARET L. and QUARRELL, W. H., *Lichtenberg's Visits to England as described in his Letters and Diaries*, Oxford: Clarendon Press, 1938.

MARLOWE, JOHN, *Late Victorian. The Life of Sir Arnold Wilson*, London: Cresset Press, 1967.

MARX, KARL, *Economic and Philosophic Manuscripts of 1844*, London: Lawrence and Wichart, 1959.

MARWICK, ARTHUR, 'Middle Opinion in the Thirties', *English Historical Review*, No. 311, xxix, 1964, 285–298.

MASUR, GERHARD, 'Distinctive Traits of Western Civilization: Through the Eyes of Western Historians', *American Historical Review*, LXVII, No. 3, 1962, 591–608.

MATHESON, P. E., *German Visitors to England 1770–95 and their impressions*, Oxford: Clarendon Press, The Taylorian Lecture, 1930.

MCKIE, DOUGLAS, 'The Origins and Foundations of the Royal Society of London', *Notes and Records of the Royal Society*, XV, 1960, 1–37.

MEINEKE, F., *Geschichte des Deutsche-englischen Bündnisproblem*, Munich and Berlin: R. Olderbury, 1927.

MERKL, P. H., *Germany, Yesterday and Tomorrow*, New York: Oxford University Press, 1965.

MEUSCH, R. A., 'Goethe and Wordsworth', *Publications of the English Goethe Society*, 7, 1893.

MICKLEM, NATHANIEL, *National Socialism and the Roman Catholic Church*, Oxford: Royal Institute of International Affairs, 1939.

MINISTRY OF RECONSTRUCTION, *Adult Education Committee Final Report*, London: H.M.S.O., Cmd. 321, 1919.

Minutes of the Committee of Council on Education 1847–8, 1/11, 1848.

MITFORD, NANCY, 'Augustus Hare 1834–1903', *Horizon*, vi (1942), 322–8.

MONROE, W. S., *The Pestalozzian Movement in the United States*, Syracuse, N.Y., 1907.

MONTGOMERY, J. D., *Forced to be Free: The Artificial Revolution in Germany and Japan*, Chicago: University of Chicago Press, 1957.

MOORHOUSE, SYDNEY, *Walking Tours and Hostels in England*, London, Country Life, 1936.

MORGAN, B. Q., and HOHLFELD, A. R. (Ed.), *German Literature in British Magazines 1750–1860*, Madison: University of Wisconsin Press, 1949.

MORGAN, B. Q., *German Frequency Word Book*, Publication of the American and Canadian Committee on Modern Languages, vol. 9, 1928.

MORLEY, E. J., *Crabb Robinson in Germany, 1800–1805*, London: Humphrey Milford, 1929.

MORLEY, JOHN, *Life of Gladstone*, London: Edward Lloyd Ltd., 1908.

MORYSON, FYNES, *An Itinerary, Containing His Ten Yeeres Travell through the Twelve Dominions of Germany, Bohmerland, Swetzerland, Netherland, Denmarke, Poland, Italy, Turky, France, England, Scotland and Ireland*, Glasgow: James MacLehose and Sons, 1907–8 (orig. 1617).

MOSSE, W. E., *The European Powers and the Germans 1848–1871*, Cambridge: University Press, 1958.

MUGGERIDGE, MALCOLM, 'Then and Now', *Encounter*, xxii (1964), pp. 20–22.

MUGGERIDGE, MALCOLM, *The Thirties 1930–1940 in Great Britain*, London: Collins, 1967.

MUIR, PERCY, *English Children's Books 1600–1900*, London: B. T. Batsford, 1954.

MUMBY, F. A., *The House of Routledge 1834–1934, with a history of Kegan Paul, Trench, Trübner and other associate firms*, London: G. Routledge, 1934.

MUMBY, F. A., *Publishing and Bookselling from the Earliest Times to the Present Day*, London: Jonathan Cape, 1956.

MUSGRAVE, P. W., *Technical Change and the Labour Force in Education. A Study of the British and German Iron and Steel Industries 1860–1964*, London: Pergamon Press, 1967.

MUSSON, A. E., *Enterprise in Soap and Chemicals. Joseph Crosfield and Sons Limited, 1815–1965*, Manchester: University Press, 1965.

NATIONAL UNION OF STUDENTS, *The German Singers. An Account of Some British German Activities 1928–1930*, London: National Union of Students, 1931.

NEMNICH, P. A., *Description of a Journey from Hamburg to England and of a Journey through England in the Summer of 1799*, 1800.

NESBITT, G. I., *Benthamite Reviewing: the First Twelve Years of the 'Westminster Review' 1824–1836*, New York: Columbia University Studies in English and Comparative Literature, No. 118, 1934.

NORMAN, F., 'H .C. Robinson and Goethe', *Publications of the English Goethe Society*, N.S. 6, 1930.

NORTON, LORD, ' "Cramming" in Elementary Schools', *The Nineteenth Century*, xv, 1884, 262–273.

ODY, H. J., *Begegnung zwischen Deutschland, England und Frankreich im höheren Schulwesen seit Beginn des 19. Jahrhunderts*, Saarbrücken: Gesellschaft für bildendes Schrifttum, 1959.

OGDEN, C. K. (trans.), *The Schools and the Nation by George Kerschensteiner*, London: Macmillan & Co., 1914.

OPIE, R. E., 'Western Germany's Economic Miracle', *The Three Banks Review*, March 1962.

ORWELL, GEORGE, *Collected Essays*, London: Mercury Books, No. 17, 1966.

124

PAULSEN, FRIEDRICH, *German Education, Past and Present*, London: T. F. Unwin, 1908.

PAYNE, JOSEPH, *A visit to German Schools: Notes of a Professional Tour*, London: Henry King, 1876.

PEARSON, H. N., *Memoirs of the Life and Correspondence of Christian Frederich Swartz*, London, 1834.

PERRY, W. C., *German University Education or the Professors and Students of Germany, to which is added a brief account of the public schools of Prussia with observations on the influence of philosophy on the studies of German Universities*, London: Longman, Brown, Green and Longmans, 1846.

PEVSNER, NICOLAUS, 'English and German Art and their interrelations', *German Life and Letters*, ii, 1937–8, 251–259.

PFLANZE, OTTO, *Bismarck and the Development of Germany. The Period of Unification 1815–1871*, Princeton, New Jersey: Princeton University Press, 1963.

PINSON, KOPPEL S., *Modern Germany Its History and Civilisation*, 2nd edn., London: Collier-Macmillan, 1966.

POCHMANN, HENRY, A., *German Culture in America: Philosophical and Literary Influences 1800–1900*, Madison: University of Wisconsin Press, 1957.

POPE-HENNESSY, JAMES, *Monckton Milnes*, London: Constable, 1949.

PRICE, L. M., *The Reception of English Literature in Germany*, Berkeley: University of California Press, 1932.

QUIGLEY, H. and CLARK, R. T., *Republican Germany*, New York: Dodd, Mead and Co., 1928.

RAUMER, FRIEDRICH VON, *England in 1841* (transl. by H. Evans Lloyd), London: J. Lee, 1842.

REDLICH, F., 'Academic Education for Business: Its Development and the Contribution of Ignaz Jastrow 1856–1937,' *Business History Review*, XXXI (1), 1957.

REED, BERTA, *The Influence of Solomon Gessner on English Literature*, Philadelphia: 1905.

REHLING, A. W., 'Collegiate Education for Business in Germany', *Journal of Political Economy*, XXXIV (L926) 545.

Report of Assistant Commissioners Appointed to Inquire into the State of Popular Education in Continental Europe and on Educational Charity in England and Wales 1861, Vol. IV, London: H.M.S.O. (St.), pp. 161–266.

BIBLIOGRAPHY

Report of Select Committee on Scientific Instruction of U.S.A. Commissioner of Education for the Year 1899–1900, Washington: Government Printing Office, 1901, vol. 2, 1867–8.

Report of Royal Commission on the Depression of Trade and Industry, London: H.M.S.O., 1886.

First report of Royal Commissioners on Technical Instruction, 1882, London: H.M.S.O., 1882–3171

RICH, R. W., *The Training of Teachers*, Cambridge: University Press, 1933.

ROBERTS, STEPHEN H., *The House that Hitler Built*, London: Methuen, 1937.

ROBBINS, WILLIAM, *The Ethical Idealism of Matthew Arnold*, London: William Heinemann, 1959.

ROLL-HANSEN, DIDERIK, *The Academy 1869–1879: Victorian Intelligentsia in Revolt*, Copenhagen, 1957.

ROSE, F., *Commercial Instruction in Germany*, Foreign Office Series of Diplomatic and Consular Reports No. 619, London: Eyre and Spottiswoode, 1904.

ROWSE, A. L., *All Souls and Appeasement*, London: Macmillan and Co., 1961.

RUSK, R. F., *The Training of Teachers in Scotland*, Edinburgh: The Educational Institute of Scotland, 1928.

RUSSELL, G. W. E., *Letters of Matthew Arnold 1848–1888*, London: Macmillan and Co., 1901.

RUSSSELL, J. F., 'History of the Hallé Concerts', *Hallé Magazine*, X, 18.

RYE, WILLIAM BRENCHLEY, *England as seen by Foreigners*, London: John Russell Smith, 1865.

SADLER, MICHAEL, *Continuation Schools in England and Elsewhere*, Manchester: University Press, 1907.

SADLER, M., *Die Neueren Sprachen*, Band XX, H. 6, 1912, 321–5.

SADLER, M., *The History of Education in Germany in the Nineteenth Century*, Manchester: University Press, 1915, 103–127.

SAMUEL, R. H. and HINTON, THOMAS R., *Education and Society in Modern Germany*, London: Routledge & Kegan Paul, 1949.

SCHAIBLE, K. H., *Geschichte der Deutschen in England von den ersten germanischen Ansiedlungen in Britannien bis zum Ende des 18. Jahrhunderts*, Strassburg: Trübner, 1885.

SCHAIBLE, K. H., *The State and Education*, London: E. Stanford, 1870.

SCHAIBLE, K. H., *The Theory and Practice of Teaching Modern Languages in Schools*, London: Trench, Trübner, 1869

SCHAIRER, REINHOLD and HOFFMAN, CONRAD, J., *Das Universitäts-ideale der Kultur vollker*, Leipzig: Quelle and Meyer, 1925.

SCHMIDT, 'The Hessian Mercenaries: the career of a political cliché, *History* 48 (1958), 207–12.

SCHNABEL, FRANZ, *Die Anfänge des technischen Hochschulwesens*, Karlsrühe: Buchdruckerei, C. F. Müller, 1925.

SCHNEIDER, FRIEDRICH, *Geltung und Einflluss der Deutschen Pädagogik im Ausland*, Munich and Berlin: R. Oldenburg, 1943.

SCHOENBAUM, DAVID, *Hitler's Social Revolution*, London: Weidenfeld and Nicolson, 1967.

SCHULZ, F., *Die Hanse und England von Edwards III bis auf Heinrichs VIII Zeit*, Berlin: 1911.

SCOTT, D. F. S., 'Sarah Austin and Germany', *German Life and Letters*, N.S.2, 1948–9, 138–143.

SCOTT, D. F. S., 'English Visitors to Weimar', *German Life and Letters*, N.S.2, 1948–9, 330–341.

SCOTT, D. F. S., *Some English Correspondents of Goethe*, London: Methuen, 1949.

SELLIER, WALTER, *Kotzebue in England. Ein Beitrag zur Geschichte der englischen Bühne und der Beziehungen der deutschen Literatur zur englischen*, Leipzig, 1901.

SHADWELL, A., *Industrial Efficiency*, London: Longmans, Green and Co., 1906.

SHANAHAN, W. D., *Prussian Military Reforms 1786–1813*, New York: Columbia University Studies in history, economics and public law No. 520, 1945.

SHANNON, R. T., 'John Robert Seeley and the Idea of a National Church' in Robson, R. (Ed.), *Ideas and Institutions of Victorian Britain*, London: G. Bell and Sons, 1967.

SHUMWAY, DAVID, B., 'Göttingen's American Students', *American-German Review*, iii, 1937, 21–4.

SHUMWAY,, D. B., 'Thomas Campbell and Germany', *Schelling Anniversary Papers*, New York: The Century Co., 1923.

SIMONS, DIANE, *George Kerchensteiner. His Thought and its Relevance Today*, London: Methuen, 1966.

SMITH, SIR SWIRE, *The Real German Rivalry: yesterday, today and tomorrow*, London: T. F. Unwin, 1916 and 1918.

SMITH, SIR SWIRE, *Educational Comparisons, or remarks on Industrial Schools in England, Germany and Switzerland*, London and Bradford: Simpkin, Marshall and Co., 1873.

SMITHELLS, ARTHUR, 'German Science', in *From a Modern University*, Oxford: University Press, 1921, 95–124.

SNEYD-KYNNERSLEY, *H.M.I. Some Passages in the Life of one of H.M. Inspectors of Schools*. London : John Lane, The Bodley Head Ltd., 1930.

SOMMER, DUDLEY, *Haldane of Cloan*, London : George Allen and Unwin, 1960.

SONTAG, R. J., *Germany and England: Background of Conflict 1848–1918*, New York : D. Appleton—Century Co., 1938.

SPARROW, JOHN, *Mark Pattison and the Idea of a University*, Cambridge : University Press, 1967.

Special Reports on Educational Subjects, 1, 3, 9, 19, 20 and 22, London : H.M.S.O., 1896–7, 1898, 1902, 1907, 1909.

STAHL, E. L., 'Das erste deutsche lektorat in England', *Die Neueren sprachen*, 18, 1910–11, 25–33.

STANLEY, A. P., *The Life and Correspondence of Thomas Arnold D.D.*, London : Ward, Lock, 1890.

STEEL, SIR CHRISTOPHER, 'Anglo-German Relations : A Retrospective Look', *International Affairs*, October, 1963.

STELLE, GÖTZ VON, *Die Georg August Universität zu Göttingen*, Göttingen : Vanvenhoeck and Ruprecht, 1937.

STEPHEN, LESLIE, 'The Importation of German', *Studies of a Biographer*, II, 1898.

STERNFELD, WILHELM and TIEDIEMANN, *Deutsche Exil-Literatur 1933–1945*, Heidelberg : Darmstadt Verlag Lambert 1962, Schneider.

STIRK, S. D., *German Universities—Through English Eyes*, London : Victor Gollancz, 1946.

STOKOE, F. W., *German Influence in the English Romantic Period 1788–1818 with special reference to Scott, Coleridge, Shelley and Byron*, Cambridge : University Press, 1926.

STOLPER, GUSTAV, *German Economy 1870–1940: Issues and Trends*, New York : Reynal and Hitchcock, 1940.

STORR, M., *The Relation of Carlyle to Kant and Fichte*, Bryn Mawr : 1929.

STOYE, J. W., *English Travellers Abroad 1604–1667. Their influence in English society and politics*, London : Jonathan Cape, 1952.

STRUVE, WALTER, 'Hans Zehrer as a Neoconservative Élite Theorist', *American Historical Review*, LXX, pt. 2, 1965, 1035–1057.

SUPER, R. H., *The Complete Prose Works of Matthew Arnold, Schools and Universities on the Continent*, Ann Arbor, Michigan : Michigan University Press, 1964–6. 6 vols.

SYKES, N., *Daniel Ernst Jablonski and the Church of England*, London: S.P.C.K., 1950.

TAYLOR, JAMES, *Remarks on the German Empire*, London: 1745.

TERRES, E., (Ed.) *Festrede bei d. Gedenkfeier d. 125 jährigen Bestehens d. Technische Hochschule Karlsruhe:* Essen, Girardet, 1950.

The German Singers. An account of Some British German Activities 1928–1930, London: National Union of Students, 1931.

THIRLWALL, JOHN CONNOP, *The Life of Connop Thirlwall*, London: S.P.C.K., 1936.

THIRLWALL, J. C., *The Present State of relations between Science and Literature—an address*, London: 1867. *Letters to a Friend*, Ed. A. P. Stanley, London: Bentley and Son, 1881.

THOMAS, A. W., *A History of Nottingham High School, 1513–1953*, Nottingham: H. Bell, 1957.

THOMAS, BRINLEY, *Economics of International Migration*, London: Macmillan, 1958.

THOMPSON, JOSEPH, *The Owens College: its foundation and growth*, Manchester: J. E. Cornish, 1886.

THOMPSON, JAMES WESTFALL, *Economic and Social History of Europe in the later Middle Ages (1300–1530)*, New York: The Century Co., 1931.

THWING, CHARLES F., *The American and the German University*, New York: The Macmillan Company, 1928.

TODT, W., 'Lessing in England, *Anglistische Arbeiten*, ed. L. L. Schüking, Heidelberg, 1912.

TREASE, GEOFFREY, *The Grand Tour*, London: Heinemann, 1967.

TWENTYMAN, A. E., '*The Earlier History of Technical High Schools in Germany*', *Special Reports on Educational Subjects*, London: H.M.S.O., IX, 1902.

ULAM, A. B., *The Philosophical Foundations of English Socialism*, New York: Octagon Books, 1964.

U.S.A. *Report of the Commissioner of Education for the year 1899–1900*, Washington: Government Printing Office, 1901, vol. ii.

VAUGHAN, C. E., *Carlyle and his German Masters*, London: English Association Essays and Studies, 1910.

VERMEIL, EDMOND, *Doctrinaires de la revolution allemande 1918–1938*, Paris, 1938.

VIËTOR, WILLIAM, *Elements of Phonetics: English, French and German*, London: Dent's Modern Language Series 1899. [Viëtor was a prolific and influential writer whose words were adopted for English students by Laura Soames]

VINCENT, ODETTE, *Un enquête économique la France Impériale: Le Voyage du Hambourgeois Philippe-Andre Nemrich*, Paris: Libraire Plon, 1947.

WAGMAN, FREDERICK HERBERT, *Magic and Natural Science in German Baroque Literature*, New York: Columbia University Press, 1942.

WALLACE, DONALD MACKENZIE, *Russia*, London: Cassell and Company, 1877.

WALZ, JOHN A., *German Influence in American Education and Culture*, Philadelphia: 1936, Carl Schutz Memorial Foundation.

WARD, A. W., *Great Britain and Hanover*, Oxford: University Press 1899.

WARD, A. W., *The Hanoverian Succession: Some Aspects,* Oxford. University Press, 1899.

WARD, W. R., *Georgian Oxford*, Oxford: Clarendon Press, 1958.

WATERFALL, E. A., *The Day Continuation School in England: its function and future*, London: George Allen and Unwin, 1923.

WATT, D. C., *Britain Looks to Germany: British Opinion and Policy towards Germany since 1945*, London: Oswald Wolff, 1965.

WEBER, C. A., 'Literarisches Bristol, Seine Bedeutung fur den provinziellen Ursprung der Englischen Romantik und für die deutsch-englischen Beziehungen', *Studien zur Englischen Philologie*, Halle, 1955.

WEIL, E., 'Samuel Browne, Printer to the University of Heidelberg 1655–1662', *The Library*, Fifth Series, 1951, 14–24.

WEIL, E., 'William Fitzer, the Publisher of Harvey's De Cordis', *The Libary*, Fourth Series, XXIX, 1944, 142–164.

WIESE, LEOPOLD, *German Letters on Education* (transl. by W. D. Arnold), London, 1854.

WHITE, JOHN, 'West German Aid to Developing Countries', *International Affairs*, Jan. 1965.

WHITFIELD, G., *A Collection of Hymns for Social Worship*, London: V. Strachan and Sold at the Tabernacle, 1753. [This went to 33 editions in almost as many years]

WILKIE, J. R., 'Goethe's English Friend Lupton', *German Life and Letters*, ix, 1955–6, 29–39.

WILLCOX, WALTER F., *International Migrations*, New York: National Bureau of Economic Research, 1931.

WILLETT, JOHN, *The Theatre of Bertolt Brecht*, London: Methuen, 1964.

WILLIAMS, E. E., 'Made in Germany', Jan-Feb, *New Review*, vol. 14, Jan-June, 1896; "Made in Germany—Five Years Later', *New Review*, vol. 38, 1901.

WILLOUGHBY, L. A., *D. G. Rossetti and German Literature, A Lecture*, Oxford: Henry Frowde, 1912.

WILLOUGHBY, L. A., 'Goethe looks at the English', *Modern Language Review*, 50, Oct. 1955.

WILLOUGHBY, L. A., 'Coleridge and his German Contemporaries', *Publication of the English Goethe Society*, N.S. 10, 1934.

WILLOUGHBY, L. A., 'Wordsworth and Germany', *German studies presented to H. G. Fiedler*, Oxford: University Press, 1937.

WILSON, E. C., *Catherine Isabella Dodd 1860–1932*, London: Sidgwick and Jackson, 1936.

WILSON, ARNOLD, *The Diary of an M.P. 1934–36*, London. Oxford University Press, 1936.

WINSTANLEY, D. A., *Unreformed Cambridge*, Cambridge: University Press, 1940.

WINSTANLEY, D. A., *Early Victorian Cambridge*, Cambridge: University Press, 1940.

WOODWARD, E. L., *Great Britain and the German Navy*, Oxford: Clarendon Press, 1935.

YOUNG, KENNETH, *Arthur James Balfour*, London: G. Bell and Son, 1963.

ZEMAN, S. A. B., *Nazi Propaganda*, London: Oxford University Press, 1964.